THE PRINCETON REVIEW

DON'T BE A CHUMP!

OTHER BOOKS IN THE PRINCETON REVIEW SERIES

Cracking the New SAT and PSAT
Cracking the New SAT and PSAT with Sample Tests on Computer Disk
Cracking the ACT
Cracking the LSAT
Cracking the LSAT with Sample Tests on Computer Disk
Cracking the GRE
Cracking the GRE with Sample Tests on Computer Disk
Cracking the GRE Psychology Test
Cracking the GMAT
Cracking the GMAT with Sample Tests on Computer Disk
Cracking the MCAT
Cracking the SAT II: Biology Subject Test
Cracking the SAT II: Chemistry Subject Test
Cracking the SAT II: English Subject Tests
Cracking the SAT II: French Subject Test
Cracking the SAT II: History Subject Tests
Cracking the SAT II: Math Subject Tests
Cracking the SAT II: Physics Subject Test
Cracking the SAT II: Spanish Subject Test
Cracking the TOEFL with audiocassette
How to Survive Without Your Parents' Money
Grammar Smart
Math Smart
Reading Smart
Study Smart
Writing Smart
Student Access Guide to America's Top 100 Internships
Student Access Guide to College Admissions
Student Access Guide to the Best Business Schools
Student Access Guide to the Best Law Schools
Student Access Guide to the Best Medical Schools
Student Access Guide to the Best 309 Colleges
Student Access Guide to Paying for College
Word Smart: Building an Educated Vocabulary
Word Smart II: How to Build a More Educated Vocabulary

ALSO AVAILABLE ON CASSETTE FROM LIVING LANGUAGE

Grammar Smart
Word Smart
Word Smart II

THE PRINCETON REVIEW

DON'T BE A CHUMP!

NEGOTIATING SKILLS YOU NEED

BY NICK SCHAFFZIN

Random House, Inc.
New York 1995

Library of Congress Cataloging-in-Publication Data

Schaffzin, Nicholas Reid.
Don't be a chump! : negotiating skills you need / Nicholas Reid
Schaffzin. -- 1st ed.
p.   cm.

ISBN 0-679-76130-6 (pbk.) : $12.00

1. Negotiation. 2. Interpersonal relations.   I. Title.
BF637 .N4S   1995
302.3--dc20

Manufactured in the United States of America on recycled paper

9 8 7 6 5 4 3 2

ACKNOWLEDGMENTS

I would like to thank Leland Elliott, Kristin Fayne-Mulroy, John Katzman, Chris Kensler, Meher Khambata, Illeny Maaza, Maria Russo, and P.J. Waters for their help and good advice in the creation and production of this book.

For their encouragement and unwavering faith, I am indebted to both Marney Mesch and Sara Reid Plumb. A special thanks goes to Beth Young for her support, her intelligent criticism, and her belief in me.

CONTENTS

Introduction

You negotiate all the time, and you don't even know it.

Sure, some things you do look and feel like negotiations—buying a new car, signing a lease for an apartment, signing a purchasing agreement—because one party wants a higher price and another party wants a lower price. They state their price, you state your price, and, if you're lucky, you reach an agreement. This book will demonstrate how to get a better price when you negotiate, point out the tricks other people might try to use on you and, most of all, show you how to avoid being a chump.

But if that's all you get out of this book, you've missed some great opportunities to make your whole life better—and *that's* a chump thing to do. Agreeing on a price is just one aspect of negotiation, and often not the first issue you want to address. One goal of this book is to make you aware of all the negotiations that go on around you and to teach you how to get the most out of every single one. When you and a friend debate what movie you want to see, that's negotiating. When you decide how much you want to spend for dinner, you're negotiating with yourself. When you subscribe to a long-distance service or a credit card, that's negotiation too. The sooner you learn to recognize that negotiating is a part of any choice, and the sooner you realize that nearly anything is negotiable, the better off you'll be. A good negotiator is never a chump.

What is a chump, anyway? Simply put, a chump is someone who accepts what is offered to him. A chump accepts everything at face value. Because chumps are afraid or disdainful of negotiating, they miss easy opportunities to get what they really want, and are never really satisfied with what they get in the end. We think people should be happy with the outcome every time they negotiate. In many cases, this will mean that you have more time, more options—and, of course, more money.

It seems like it would be obvious when you're getting a good deal and when you're getting a bad one, but it's not. And if it's difficult to tell if you've gotten a good deal, it's downright impossible to tell if you've gotten the best deal. You think, "I'm happy with what they offered. Why should I ask for more?" Even when you think you can't get any more out of a prospective seller, you owe it to both of you to find out if any more value could be found in the deal. The only way to find out what each of you values the most is negotiation.

Don't think you've been offered a good deal because the other side says it's the most "fair" offer around. You have no idea what pressure the seller faces in selling his product, or what pressure the buyer is under to buy. Perhaps the car salesman's been told if he doesn't make this sale, he's out of a job. Perhaps the real estate agent's been told if she doesn't buy your land from you, a million-dollar deal will be lost. If you come to an agreement after negotiating, you're much more likely to know for sure how the other side values the deal. Once you've negotiated, you can decide whether or not you've gotten a good deal.

Don't Be a Chump tells you how to prepare for a negotiation, how to read the people you're negotiating with, and how to decide when it's alright to walk away. Normally, it would take years of negotiating experience to get this much insight into the process. Luckily, you've got this book to give you a shortcut.

We've taken the most useful techniques from some of the best negotiators and organized them into an easy to follow, step-by-step book that teaches the skills that will make you a better negotiator. Here you will find information on how to use negotiating tactics and gambits to your advantage—and how to recognize when they're being used against you. We'll also show you how to use communication, information, and timing to your advantage. We cover the most important aspects of any negotiation from start to finish, including how to maintain a good relationship with the people you negotiate with.

What will this book do for you? Well, you should see results in your wallet. That's always welcome. But smart negotiation has many other benefits. Strong, honest, lasting relationships, less anxiety, and a general sense of contentment all should emerge once you strengthen your negotiating skills. From deciding where you should go for dinner to selling your car, these techniques will improve your quality of life.

But these techniques work only if you use them in everyday situations. And, like anything else, they work better the more you use them. Try them out, get comfortable with them, learn not only how to use them, but how to use them confidently. Negotiation may not be something you look forward to now, but soon enough you'll relish the chance to use your new and powerful skills.

If a better life, more money in your wallet, and a higher degree of fulfillment sound good to you, read this book carefully. Pay special attention to the "Negotiation Tactic Boxes" scattered throughout chapters 1 through 6. Work through the "Negotiating Workshop" exercises throughout the book and "The Negotiation Arena" in chapter 11. Try out the techniques we describe. It may be helpful to have a partner with a copy of the book, so you have someone to practice your skills with. It's always a good idea to try things out before there's any real money at stake.

Think of this book as your best line of defense. In most negotiations there's someone who takes less than she should have, who pays more than she wanted to, or who feels that if he were only a little bit better at negotiating, he would have felt much more satisfied with the outcome.

Take to heart the old poker adage: "If you've been sitting at a poker table for five hands, and you can't figure out who the chump is, it's you."

CHAPTER 1

The Basis of Negotiation

"Good morning, Sandy's Shoe Store."

"Hello, Sandy? My name's Mike. I'm looking for some Gerardi leather shoes."

"Well, Mike, you're in the right place. We sell Gerardi shoes for $69 a pair, but you sound nice, so I'll sell them to you for $49. Also, we have another brand that is exactly like Gerardi but less expensive. They go for $39 a pair."

"Gee, Sandy, you've been helpful. I want to be fair, though, so why don't you sell me the less expensive shoes, but I'd feel better if you'd let me pay $55. That way I'd feel like I was rewarding you for your good service."

"Oh, Mike, I couldn't let you do that. Why don't we split the difference? I'll sell you the real Gerardi shoes for $59 a pair. Does that sound good to you?"

"I'd love to pay that. Send them over."

Wouldn't it be wonderful if every negotiation resulted in a perfectly fair solution, fulfilling to every party involved? Wouldn't it be great if someone asked us to pay less instead of more than what we offered? Wouldn't it be great if everyone gave us all the information we needed to make an accurate and informed decision?

How many times have you been involved in a negotiation like the one between Mike and Sandy? If it's happened to you even once, you've led a charmed life. We're not saying that most people don't want to be fair. Actually, and perhaps surprisingly, most people do. At the same time, if they had a chance, most people wouldn't want to pay more than they could have, or accept less than they were offered. As painful as it is to say it, most people would not want to be like Mike. Or like Sandy, for that matter.

It's true Mike and Sandy are both fulfilled by the deal they've reached, because they both got what they wanted—for Mike, the shoes, for Sandy, the money—and they both feel like they've been fair to the other person. But the reason this seems like a fantasy is that neither Mike nor Sandy place value on having more money. Sandy seems to have no interest in keeping her store afloat, and Mike seems to want to pay more money for an inferior product.

In real life, negotiations like Mike and Sandy's just don't happen. Most likely, Mike would call Sandy up, she'd let him know the price, and if he were serious about buying the shoes, he'd come down

1

Good Cop/Bad Cop

Identification
Two people are negotiating for one side, and one of them appears to be stern and outrageously demanding, while the other tries to befriend you. They work in conjunction to disorient you. While the nasty one reduces your aspiration level, the good guy tries to get valuable information from you and comfort you with every conciliation you make.

Note
This ploy was made famous by the police department, initially in Boston, where prisoners would be interrogated by two police officers employing this technique. One officer would threaten the most dire consequences the law could offer and, although illegal, suggest that physical harm would come to the person if he didn't cooperate. The other policeman would traditionally offer sustenance (food, drink, cigarettes, etc.) and have private talks with the alleged perpetrator, sympathizing and offering more lenient treatment if the prisoner cooperated and/or confessed.

Solution
In a business negotiation, any ploy that involves acting of any sort is subject to exposure. Reveal that you see something going on. A simple "you know, the two of you seem to have some kind of communication problem. One of you wants one thing, and the other wants something else. If we should negotiate at a later time, when the two of you can coordinate your positions, just let me know. I'm available when you want to get serious." If you have to, tell them that this "good cop/bad cop" thing isn't going to work. People find it more difficult to play a role once they have been exposed.

to the store. He'd have to decide whether to buy the shoes or not at the price Sandy had marked them. If he liked them, he'd buy them. If he didn't, he'd leave the store. If he liked them but didn't like the price, he'd go somewhere else. This is the time-honored practice of competitive pricing—if someone can give you a better deal, that person will get your business. In the real world, Mike and Sandy's negotiation would likely go like this:

> *"Good morning, Sandy's Shoe Store."*
>
> *"Hello, Sandy? My name's Mike. I'm looking for some Gerardi leather shoes."*
>
> *"We sell those. As a matter of fact, we have some in stock."*
>
> *"And how much do they cost?"*
>
> *"$69 a pair, plus tax."*
>
> *"Do you have anything cheaper?"*
>
> *"Yes, but their quality doesn't match up to Gerardi's. We have something slightly cheaper, but, you know, you get what you pay for."*
>
> *"And you're firm about the price for the Gerardi shoes?"*
>
> *"Yes."*
>
> *"Thank you."*
>
> *"See you soon."*

Sandy is keeping some information from Mike, and Mike is keeping his reactions guarded. They discuss availability and price, and that's it. There's no negotiation here. There's an offer to sell at a pre-determined price. Mike is likely to accept or reject that price without thinking about negotiating. Mike is unlikely to think about all the benefits that could come to him from negotiating.

Negotiation lets you direct your business to those you want to do business with. Negotiation lets you dictate the parts of any deal that are important to you—price, timing, method of payment, anything that makes a difference to you. Negotiation tends to improve your fulfillment with every aspect of every deal you make. It follows that those people who negotiate better end up happier in their business and personal lives. Let's imagine Mike is a better negotiator than he was before. This negotiation might have gone like this:

"Good morning, Sandy's Shoe Store."

"Hello, Sandy? My name's Mike. I bought some sneakers and boots from you last week."

"Oh yes."

"I'm wondering about your price for some Gerardi leather shoes."

"We sell those. As a matter of fact, we have some in stock right now, if you want to pick them up today. They cost $69 a pair, plus tax."

"Yipes! I just called Dorothy's shoes down the block, and they're selling them for $55 a pair. I really love the sneakers and boots I bought from you, though, and I'd rather do business at your store—is there any way you can come down on the price?"

"I could come down to about $63, but that's as low as I could go."

"I had my mind set on spending only about $50, and I want to get these shoes today. I didn't know it was so expensive just for some nice leather shoes..."

"Do they have to be Gerardi?"

"No, just some nice leather shoes. Someone recommended Gerardi to me."

"We have something about as good as Gerardi, but for $49. You always pay a little more for a name brand."

"Really?"

"Yup. Why don't you try these other shoes and see if you like them?"

"I will. Thanks for the tips. I'll recommend your store to all my friends."

"I'd appreciate that."

By employing some simple signal-sending techniques and communicating more effectively, Mike's given himself a number of options about shoes, price, and quality. He's let Sandy know that he is a regular customer, and that if he's satisfied he will bring her even more business. Even if he and Sandy don't reach an agreement on a pair of shoes and a price, he's established a good relationship with Sandy that can only work to his advantage in the future.

Even the process of negotiating helps you feel better about any deal. Have you ever complained about prices at the supermarket? Have you said that the price of an item was outrageously high, or that you wished that there were the same number of hot dogs and hot dog buns in every package? Your unhappiness with the state of affairs at the supermarket isn't just about high prices. It stems from the idea that you have no say in the price of the item; the supermarket just sets a price and puts the product on the shelf in a "take-it-or-leave-it" fashion. You're excluded from the process of deciding the value of that item. It's not surprising that you leave the supermarket, wallet bled of cash, vaguely unhappy with the deals you didn't get.

It doesn't matter where you are—the principles of negotiation apply. In 1992 at Yale University, the graduate students who taught introductory classes formed a union to negotiate for better terms from University officials. The University refused to recognize them as a union and dismissed their requests. Other unions at Yale went on strike in support of the graduate students and, while the graduate student union remains unrecognized, their demands for higher salaries and more reasonable hours were eventually met by the administration.

Now, you've got very little choice about what you pay once you're in the supermarket. But even in buying food, you have other options. In a competitive market, there's always a way to negotiate. Are there other supermarkets in your neighborhood? Are there smaller, local stores? Can you get together with some neighbors and order food in bulk to get wholesale prices? Can you find someone willing to drive to another neighborhood where groceries are cheaper? All these options take some effort, but the result is cash that remains in your pocket.

In part, the "non-negotiating" mentality that makes people take what they are given reflects what we call "the power of the press" (see chapter 6). If you believe everything you see printed, you're going to think that what's printed is always your only option. We're asking you to look at a transaction not only from your point of view, but from the point of view of the salesperson. Many salespeople work for commission. If this is the case, then which is more important to them—keeping a price high and making very few deals, or lowering the price a little and making a lot of deals? Salespeople, generally, are more interested in making a deal than in keeping an advertised price intact. It means more money for them and more money left over for you. Yet once a price is printed on a flyer, or in an ad, or even on a tag, people assume that, like in the supermarket, the price is set in stone.

Any deal is an agreement between two parties. If you don't like the terms of your agreement (in this case, the price) you have the right to try to negotiate that term to your greater contentment. If you can't get that term to an acceptable place, then you have the right to walk away. Don't get fooled by the power of the press. You don't believe everything else you read. Why should you believe a price tag?

The moral is this: Just because a price is marked doesn't mean that's the final price you'll get. The other side, however, may want something back from you if they give up on price. This means that you should start to think about the timing of any deal and the terms of payment. These are important issues that neither side can afford to take lightly. The next time you drive down the highway, look at the gas stations and count how many of them offer a different price per gallon for gas if you pay with cash rather than by credit card. Nearly all of them will offer you a discount if you pay cash. Do you think the gas stations would offer a discount if the terms of the deal were unimportant to them? Of course not. How and when you pay are sometimes the most powerful tools you have in your negotiating arsenal.

If we can get good deals all the time, then why don't people negotiate more? The reasons people do not negotiate have nothing to do with being happy about prices or even with having limited opportunities to negotiate. The main reasons people don't negotiate are:

1. **People are lazy**

   This doesn't mean that people are bad, malicious, stupid, or unkind. It just means that, generally, if a bit of a hassle may or may not reduce the price of an object a little, most people don't think it is worth the effort. People value their peace of mind, and if they are not good at negotiation, they don't want to spend their energy on a futile task.

2. People don't like conflict

Conflict is unsettling. When you challenge a written price, you imagine it's the equivalent of calling the salesperson or the store a liar (clearly, this is not the case, but it still feels that way). Someone is going to ask you to defend your position. You are going to have to explain to a very unsympathetic audience why you think a price is too high or the terms too unappealing.

3. People don't think about negotiation

You see a price marked on a tag or get a price quoted to you and you assume it is the final price as dictated by the ruler of the universe, particularly if that price is already reduced. You then decide if you want to buy the item or not. You don't think you're allowed to ask for a reduction in price.

Most people's views about negotiation are summarized as follows: It's unpleasant, combative, often hostile, and at times, insulting. These ideas come about through a history of unpleasant or unsuccessful negotiation. As a result, most people don't like to negotiate. Carving out a deal takes energy and consideration. That's why most people don't reach the best agreements they could have. It takes time, it takes effort, and it takes skills. Even if you have the time and the desire, without those skills you're going to run into trouble. Let's look at an example. David lacks negotiating skills, and, like a moth to a candle, he's off to negotiate a car deal. David's about to get burned.

It's a hot August day, and David kicks the rear bumper of his car as he pushes it into the used car lot. He's sweating profusely, large stains spreading out from under each of his arms. Larry, the car dealer, comes out to greet him.

"Having a little car trouble?" he asks.

"You bet. I've had it with this piece of junk. I've got a meeting tomorrow seventy miles away that my job depends on. What kind of cars do you have?"

"Well," says Larry, taking off his jacket, "we're a little short in the inventory department here. Now we have this little blue one here, for about $6,000."

"I can spend six thousand. Tell me about the car," says David.

"It's been driven about, oh, 256,000 miles. On good days, it runs alright. No air conditioning, of course. But we could install it. That'd take about, say, four days."

"I don't know..."

"Or we have this green model, in excellent condition, only 17,000 miles on it."

"I'll take it."

"Well," Larry runs his hand through his hair, "it happens that I just sold it this morning. This woman from Rubeville bought it for $11,000. She's picking it up in an hour. It is a beauty, though."

"I'll give you $12,000."

Larry winces. "I've got my reputation to think of. I don't want to be known as the guy who backed out of a deal."

The sun beats down on David's shoulders. "I'll give you $14,000 for it."

Larry thinks about it. "Let me give her a call, see if she'd be willing to part with it." Larry strolls into his air-conditioned office and takes a drink of water. He picks up the phone and dials. David can see Larry through the window talking on the phone. Larry strolls out. "David, this is the best I can do for you. Now you know I'd love to give you the car—but I'm going to have to pay Mrs. Carruthers off if I want her to give up the car. The best, the absolute best I can do, David—and it's only because you're in such a bind that I'm willing to go back on my deal with Mrs. Carruthers—is if you give me $15,000. I'm not really even making a profit at those rates. As a bonus, I'll take your old car off your hands. You won't have to pay any towing fees or demolition costs."

Dave wrings his hands together as the sun heats his shoulders and forearms.

Larry points toward the cool, air-conditioned office. "If you want to sign the papers, we could go inside." Dave can see the water cooler through the window.

Dave sticks out his hand. "You've got yourself a deal."

Larry takes his hand and shakes it. "You've got yourself one hell of a car."

If any part of this scenario seems familiar to you, then you know what it's like to feel trapped and powerless in a negotiation. Unfortunately, this is the type of experience most people have with negotiations. They avoid negotiation by letting the terms be dictated to them by others, and they settle for a deal that leaves them unhappy. It's no wonder that most people have negative perceptions about the art of negotiation.

The negotiations to bring the U.S. hostages back from Iran in 1979-80 took over a year (444 days). In this high-profile negotiation, the Carter Administration committed several negotiating blunders. Perhaps the most important misstep was the failure to take into account all the negative ramifications of a protracted negotiation. The longer the negotiations dragged on, the more ineffectual Carter appeared. To make matters worse, a new flag was raised on the White House lawn for every day the hostages remained in Iran, providing a constantly growing image of Carter's failure. Effectively, those negotiations weren't just for hostages—they were for the presidency.

Considering Dave's outcome from this car negotiation, it's easy to feel that negotiation is awful. Dave is out of a lot of money and has bought a car that may or may not satisfy his needs. Larry, on the other hand, will go home to his family and keep them laughing about the terrific deal he struck today and about the sucker he got to buy that car he hadn't been able to get rid of.

You see, most people think of negotiation as conflict. They think that there is only one option—that whatever one person gains has to be wrestled from the other person's hands. The idea that "whatever I gain you must lose" is false. Negotiations cannot occur without some common interest. Dave needs a car more than he needs his cash. Larry has enough cars; he wants a sale. By having something in common, they both have an interest in negotiating.

Remember: Negotiations are based not on conflict but on commonality. The two parties have something of value to exchange with each other. Conflict is what occurs when negotiations don't go smoothly, when people don't communicate well, or when people have different ideas about the value of objects, items, or services. Conflict results from failed negotiations, not from the act of negotiating properly.

What if Dave had some negotiating skills? Do you think Dave could have reached a better agreement even while pushing his dead car into the lot? Probably. But he's putting himself at a disadvantage right away with his initial introduction to Larry. Larry knows a number of things from Dave's situation. He knows:

1. Dave's car is dead. He's going to need another one right away.
2. Dave is ready to buy another car. He's sick of the old one.
3. Dave tells him he has an *important* meeting tomorrow. He needs a car now.
4. It's hot out and Dave's hot. Dave wants this done as soon as possible.

Do you think this information works to Larry's advantage? Without question. In any negotiation, information is critical to reaching a mutually satisfying agreement. The more information you have, the more likely it is that your side will come out with a fulfilling deal (see chapter 2 for more on information). If Dave does a few simple things, like leave his dead car at home and not reveal his meeting the next day, he can greatly improve his chance of reaching a better agreement. Let's look at what would happen if Dave acquired a few of the basic negotiating skills.

> *Dave walks up to the car dealer and offers his hand. "Hi. My name's Dave, and I'm looking for a car."*
>
> *Larry shakes Dave's hand. "Good thing, Dave. I sell cars. Problem is, I've only got two on the lot right now."*
>
> *"When are you getting more cars in?"*
>
> *"Sometime this week. Do you need one right away?"*
>
> *"Not really. I'm just comparing prices. What do you have on the lot?"*
>
> *"Two cars. One's got great longevity, and the other's an air-conditioned beauty."*
>
> *"What do they sell for?"*
>
> *"The first sells for $6,000, the second for $12,000."*

"And you have nothing in between?"

"Maybe something will come in later this week."

"Do you have any financing here on the lot?"

"Sure. We've got all kind of financing."

"But I could also pay cash?"

"Son, if we didn't accept cash, I don't think we'd be much of a business."

"Is there any discount for paying it all up front?"

"We might be able to work something out."

"Let's go inside and talk about what we can do about these prices. If we can work something out, maybe we can do a deal today—an all cash deal."

"I'm not sure how far I'm willing to budge on the price, but I'll always listen to a good offer."

Dave takes a stack of bills out of his pocket and thumbs through fifty-dollar bills as he talks, counting. "Fine. And if we can't come to an agreement, then we can talk later in the week about what else has come in."

Larry stares intently at the big rectangle of cash in Dave's hand. Larry wipes his forehead. "Step inside, Dave, have a glass of water. It's hot out here."

By using a few simple techniques, Dave is going to get a much better deal than he did before. Larry still isn't a pushover, but he is less in control of the negotiation and has great incentive to modify his position. Dave managed to conceal his need, begin discussing terms, and establish a friendly rapport with the salesperson. Sounds obvious, but it's amazing how many times and in how many ways people undermine their own negotiating positions.

Prosecutors are often negotiators, getting a party to plead guilty to a lesser charge to avoid the chances and expense of trial. It is estimated that over 80% of all convictions in New York State are the result of plea bargains. It's not surprising that once arrested most people seem to want to negotiate. But it shouldn't take an arrest warrant to get you to face the negotiations in your life.

If the basis of negotiation is mutual interest, then every negotiation should be an effort to get at that mutual interest to everyone's satisfaction. If there is no way to reach that common agreement, then everyone should agree that there is no point in striking a bargain. Sometimes, as we discuss in chapter 7, no deal is the best deal.

The question is how to get that mutual interest to produce the best deal. This is where the skilled negotiator separates himself from the unskilled negotiator. The unskilled negotiator will focus only on her own interest and will direct all efforts at achieving a one-sided agreement. What will the skilled negotiator focus on?

1. Communication

More often than not, communication—speaking and listening to others with care and attention—can help you get most of what you want. You have to say exactly what you want to say, you have to anticipate how it will be heard, and you have to listen. Of these, probably the most valuable skill is listening. The key is to listen to what the other party says, and to listen as well for exactly what the other party *means*.

For example, if a landlord says, "I never rent to people under thirty," he means exactly that. But you might be able to guess at his *reasons* for not renting to people under thirty from his statement. He might be saying "I value my peace and quiet and don't want anyone who makes noise at night in this apartment." If you address his fears, you might tell him that you are a quiet, calm guy with few friends, and that you would be willing to put a "peace and quiet" clause in your lease. Perhaps this will be the first time he breaks his rule. By listening for peoples' needs, rather than merely their words, you're going to be able to offer alternatives that the other side might not have considered.

2. Strategic Education

In chapter 4 we'll discuss when you should use Strategic Education and when it will work to your disadvantage. In general, the more someone understands your reasons for disagreeing with their terms, the more likely that person is to come back to you with a more appetizing deal. Often, the person you negotiate with has a boss, to whom she is accountable. If she can go back to her boss with a list of problems you have with terms, her boss may give her more leeway to change those terms to get your business.

3. Creativity

Without some creativity, any negotiation will leave at least some of the participants unfulfilled. If a car dealer says to someone, "This car is $27,000. Take it or leave it," and he responds, "I'll give you $7,000 and not a penny more," how successful do you think this negotiation will be?

   (a) Very successful. A deal will be struck in under a minute.

   (b) Successful. A deal will be struck in under three minutes.

   (c) Unsuccessful. They are negotiating one item of the deal and both appear unwilling to negotiate.

Now, I'm not a betting man, but if I had to choose one of the answers, I think (c) is the most likely candidate. You can almost picture the two of them, standing across from each other, arms folded, each waiting for the other to cave in.

The rights to market the Pope's likeness on T-shirts, mugs, and other paraphernalia is licensed by the Vatican prior to the Pontiff's visit to the United States. The Vatican reviews carefully thousands of applicants and chooses the one who most nearly fits their spiritual, financial, and moral needs. This seems like a sure money-maker for the lucky licensee. But beware—the Pope will not allow any clause in the contract that leaves the Vatican financially responsible in the event the Pope cancels his trip. Not even Frank Sinatra could get away with that—most concert paraphernalia companies insist on a cancellation indemnification.

Creativity opens up options that allow one party's needs to be met in a way they didn't think possible. What if the buyer responded, "You know, my friend wants to buy a car just like this, and I'd like you to get the commission on that car too. Now, neither of us can pay $27,000, but what if we agreed to buy two cars from you? I bet the commission from two cars at a lower price is much better than the commission on no cars at that price." Immediately you've given the salesperson a reason to alter his position. Why? Because you've offered a creative way to change the scale of the deal, and, therefore, he no longer has to stick to his original terms.

Other parts of the deal may be negotiable as well. When are you willing to accept delivery of the car? What colors does the dealer have? Are there any demonstration models on sale? How is payment done? Do you need financing? If so, what are the terms of the financing? Is it near the end of the month? Has the salesperson had a successful month or a lousy month? Is his job on the line if he doesn't move some inventory? You're never going to know everything about every negotiation, but by paying attention and thinking creatively, you're going to get a better deal.

Keep all of these issues—communication, education, and creativity—in mind as you read this book. Even as we teach you how to identify and disarm the standard negotiating tactics that other people will try to use on you, remember the fundamental aspects of a good negotiation. The best result of any negotiation is to know that you are content, see that the other party is content, and both look forward to the next negotiation.

2 Higher Authority

Identification
You are negotiating with someone who is a representative for a company, and everything he says begins with "I'd love to, but..." because he is responsible to a higher authority. All substantive changes have to be approved by his boss. He can express sympathy and a desire to offer more, but all the hard decisions can be blamed on the boss.

Note
This ploy is, in fact, the way most large corporations and salesmen negotiate. While they do have more authority than they generally let on, most of the time, it is a true state of affairs. They do have to get unusual changes approved and they do have to explain their deals to their boss. Also, this technique can have positive repercussions: It can remove emotions from the negotiations, and let both parties focus on the problems at hand.

Solution
When this tactic makes you uncomfortable the solution is simple. Demand to negotiate with someone who has authority. Explain to your negotiating partner that he may not be able to relate to exactly what your needs are, and that you need to talk to someone in charge. A willingness to go up the ladder to face authority generally earns you points during the negotiation.

NEGOTIATING WORKSHOP #1

Test Your Skills

Take a look at the following negotiation and write down all the ways you think this negotiation between Stanley and Iris failed.

> Stanley is looking at Iris's apartment. He needs a place to rent in two weeks, when his other lease expires. He will be living on the street if he can't close a deal with Iris. He has told Iris he needs her apartment, but he doesn't say why.
>
> Iris has lived here for thirty years. She loves her apartment. She has put painstaking effort and care into maintaining and improving her apartment. However, she has seen the maintenance go up and up and she can no longer afford it. She's told Stanley that she is going to move but has not told him why.
>
> "Look at the French doors and the beautiful molding around the ceiling," says Iris.
>
> "Lovely. Now, can we talk about the closing date. I've got a meeting to get to."
>
> "But you haven't even seen the fixtures and the tile mosaic in the kitchen."
>
> Stanley scratches his head. "Do you want more money, is that what you want?"
>
> Iris looks distraught. "You didn't even notice the southern exposure."
>
> "Look," Stanley takes out his checkbook and uncaps his pen. "I'll give you $5,000 more than you want. Just name a date this week I can move my stuff in."
>
> "I'm not sure about this..."
>
> "$10,000 more."
>
> Iris looks at Stanley's twitching hand and tries to picture this man taking care of her apartment (for she truly thought of it as hers) with the same loving touch she has used for all these years. She looks at his wrinkled tie and his scuffed shoes and shakes her head no. "I'm sorry, but we don't have a deal."

"You're crazy, you're crazy," Stanley says, putting his checkbook away. "I'm willing to pay you more than the apartment is worth and you're turning it down."

Iris smiles.

CHAPTER 2

Prepare or Beware

Often, what you do before a negotiation determines how you come out of it. Your preparation before the negotiation gives you the ammunition, the armor, and the confidence to defend your position and guide your negotiating partner to your point of view. Without information, you'll find yourself overmatched by any well-prepared opponent.

Preparation doesn't just mean getting information about the other side. It means preparing a negotiation plan. By using this negotiation plan, you can be ready for any possible direction the deal may take. Anticipate your response to any situation before it happens. Then, when it does happen, you'll have a clear alternative in mind as a counterproposal. Providing the other side with options not only contributes to the substance but also adds to the tone of the negotiation. Keeping the negotiations open and flexible may lead to interesting and exciting alternatives.

Preparation is also a mindset. You have to understand what you are trying to do and know when you can walk away from the negotiations. Never go into a negotiation without any idea what you are going to do if:

1. they propose terms unacceptable to you,
2. the situation is unresolvable, or
3. they walk away from the table.

> *Here's an example of proper preparation, creative think-*
> *ing, and negotiation smarts. Dick Ebersol, NBC Sports*
> *Chief, paid $456 million for the rights to televise the 1996*
> *Olympic Games in Atlanta. He had had a conversation*
> *six months earlier with the head of the International*
> *Olympic Committee, who predicted that a $450 million*
> *bid would win the rights to televise the games. Incorpo-*
> *rating creative revenue sharing and free promotion*
> *ideas, Ebersol's bid was valued at much more than its*
> *stated $456 million. Why $456 million? "I always like to*
> *be one million above a zero or a five, because I think*
> *people always think of bids in zeros or fives," he said.*

If the first time you think of these things is when you're shaking hands with the other side right before your negotiation, you are going to leave that room with less money and worse terms than you imagined. Rest assured that the other side has gone in prepared for these contingencies.

Consider the following example of prenegotiation preparation. Randy Scrubb is the owner of the Meadeville Confederates, a major-league baseball team. He is negotiating the contract of Victor "Wheels" Kelly, their star player. Victor is being represented by Patty Rigs, an agent to many professional ballplayers of considerable note.

"Good afternoon, Ms. Rigs."

"Good afternoon, Mr. Scrubb. Let me begin by saying that my client respects your organization, has enjoyed the time he's spent here, and looks forward to the best offer you can make."

"Well, thank you, Ms. Rigs. I have enjoyed Wheels's play for the past three years and so have the fans. Let's get down to it. I'm willing to offer Wheels $900,000 for three more years. I think that's a fair deal, and I've drawn up a contract with that figure. If you'll sign right away, I've got his first payment and signing bonus, $50,000 in cash right here to hand over." Randy opens a suitcase stuffed with a thousand fifty dollar bills. Victor's eyes widen. He reaches forward to touch the money.

Patty grabs Victor's arm. "While we appreciate your generous offer, we'd like you to look at other players who have similar statistics, who are of a similar age, and who were also free agents when they signed a contract with their team. If you look at this *list of twenty other center fielders, the average salary is $800,000 per year."*

"Eight hundred thousand dollars!" Randy slams the briefcase of money shut. "That's highway robbery. I don't even get that much in salary from my company. Here I was, willing to negotiate in good faith, cash in hand, and you come back at me with insane requests? Haven't I been a fair owner to you? Didn't I give you as much time as you needed to take care of your sister when she had that skiing accident?" Randy loosens his tie. Victor nods.

Quietly, Patty continues. "And my client appreciated that. When he returned, he batted .368. He led the league in batting from that point on. Mr. Scrubb, we don't want anything more than we're due. Do you know how long the average player plays baseball?"

"Oh, the great ones play a long time..."

"Three point four years. Most players retire because of an injury. Even if they don't retire after that point, they never can play at the level or command the salary they once could have. Do you know how many other teams need a premium center fielder? Eight. Including your rivals, the Iron City Rangers."

"You wouldn't dare sign with the Rangers!"

"We'd rather sign here. You've been a great owner. Wheels has a wonderful home, and there's nothing like the Confederate fans. But we can't talk about three years at $300,000 per year. We're not trying to get anything more than we're due. If you can give us some reason that Wheels, a team leader, a batting leader, and a fielding leader, should accept less rather than more than the average, please let us know."

"Let me talk to my accountants. I'm sure we can do better."

"We'd appreciate it."

Who do you think prepared more effectively for the above negotiation? Who do you think came out better from the negotiation? Patty's job depends on knowing the industry and the fair value of her client. Sometimes a deal can look very appealing, but when you know a little more about the marketplace, you can see that you should get a much better deal. Patty did, and the dollar signs are climbing in Wheels's favor. Patty does a number of things well in this negotiation, and we'll discuss them further in chapter 7, "The Main Event."

Did Randy do anything wrong? No. But there were preparation and communication issues he could have handled better. He should have prepared more for Patty's counter-offer. He could have explained the club's position on salaries. He could have had ready some figures on the net profits of the Meadeville Confederates. He could have emphasized the family nature of the Confederates and made Wheels think of his relationships with his teammates. He had a number of options open to him at the beginning of the negotiation that are now unavailable, because he began the negotiation with a quick, uninformed attempt to snatch Victor Kelly at a low price. He established the tone and direction of the negotiations—let's talk price, period. By jumping to that area first and not setting the stage by describing the benefits of being a member of the Meadeville Confederates, Randy turned this into a one-issue negotiation—which side can get the better price. Let me repeat that Randy hasn't done anything wrong. But he also hasn't done much right. When this deal is over, he'll blame Victor, Patty, his advisors, anyone but himself. With better preparation, he might have reached a more satisfying deal.

Before any negotiation, you need to do three things: gather information, prepare a negotiation plan, and feel confident. By sepa-

3   *"Take it or Leave it"*

Identification

This is simple, basic hardball. Someone gives you an offer and says that there can be no changes—that either you accept this deal, or further negotiations are pointless.

Note

A dangerous ploy. If you use this yourself, you may come up empty-handed. If you make a statement like this and the other side rejects it, and you don't walk away, you have lost your credibility. When you lose credibility, the other side can dictate terms to you without fear of reprisal, knowing that you will never walk away from the deal.

Solution

There are two solutions that make sense. The first is to explore the possibility that they mean something other than what they've said. A "take it or leave it" offer is usually made as a "best offer," meaning that they can't go any lower on these specific terms. Ask them whether they would listen to alternative solutions if the terms changed. Most people will. The second response is what you should always be willing to do in these cases—take them at their word. Ask yourself, "is this deal one that I can accept in its present form and be happy with?" Are you going to feel unfulfilled with this agreement? If you are, be prepared to walk away.

rating your preparation into these easy categories, you'll see that getting ready for a negotiation is no more complicated than getting ready for a date. You'd know it right away if you forgot to brush your teeth, comb your hair, or put on your pants. In the same way, if you don't pay attention to any of these categories before you negotiate, you can be sure things won't go well.

Gathering Information

Sometimes, a negotiation will be helped by getting market or factual information on a subject before you begin. Find out what other people are paying and what other people are getting in similar situations. For example, let's say you are trying to rent an apartment. Some information you may want to gather before you negotiate would include:

1. What other apartments in the building are renting for.
2. What comparable apartments in the neighborhood are renting for.
3. What comparable apartments are asking as a security deposit.
4. What other apartments offer in terms of view.
5. The history of maintenance in the building.
6. The satisfaction of the other tenants in the building.
7. What the other tenants are like in the building.
8. If the other tenants have pets.
9. If there are stores/facilities near the apartment.
10. What the noise levels in the neighborhood are.
11. What the parking situation in the neighborhood is.
12. If there is a broker, how she is paid.
13. If there is a broker, whether she lives in the neighborhood.
14. What kind of security the building has.

Now, not all of these things are going to be issues you care about. But you have to know them for a number of reasons. First, you need to know them in case the other side brings them up to support their argument. For example, the landlord may say, "We're the only apartment building where every apartment comes with air conditioning." If you can tell him that you've seen three other apartments on the same block that made that same claim, you've undermined his argument for a higher rent. A landlord may tell you that they have a new boiler in the building, but if you've heard that there was no heat in the building for a month last winter, you might be able to include a clause in your lease stating that if there is no heat, you won't have to pay rent. Or, suppose your landlord pulls a New York favorite and says, "I know that this rent is higher than what you want. But I'll tell you what. I'll pay all the water bills, O.K.?" You think he's being fair and equitable—until you realize that in New York, all landlords must provide water free of charge to all renters.

By gathering factual information about the product you want to purchase, the person you're negotiating with, and the situation that surrounds your negotiation, you can exact better terms. When you don't know as much as you can before you enter negotiations, you leave yourself vulnerable to the other party's telling you things that aren't true and that mislead you.

In the event that you don't have the time or the resources to research carefully the industry statistics or the objective basis of any agreement, you have one more line of defense: *Ask the other side where they get their numbers*. By making them explain their reasoning, you will, at a minimum, get to see any way in which they skewed the figures they present to their advantage. If you can prepare independently, though, do. The best defense against information meant to mislead is prior preparation.

Preparing a Negotiation Plan

Anticipating the other side's needs and requests will put you in a strong position to respond to their demands. To do this, you need to form a negotiation plan. This plan doesn't have to come in a single form or be as rigid as a steel beam. It should be a useful "cheat sheet" of information that helps you through the most basic twists and turns of the negotiation. If a negotiation is going well, you should expect the other side to come up with options you hadn't anticipated. That's when things get fun.

The first thing you should do is write down your understanding of the other side's needs. Write down anything you believe may be important to the other side. Don't limit yourself. You're never going to show this list to anyone, and you can cross anything out that seems on second thought completely ridiculous. For example, your list in the negotiation with the landlord might read:

- Wants a renter to begin paying rent immediately
- Wants large security deposit
- Wants stable tenant
- Wants trouble-free tenant

Then, write down a list of all the things you believe the other side will ask for. In the landlord case, the list may read like this:

- Lease begins on the first of the month
- Two month's rent as security deposit
- Lease for one year only
- No pets
- $900 per month rent

This list is only your first guess as to what the other side will initially demand. Obviously, as the negotiation progresses, your understanding of the other side's needs will change. Making the list is merely a springboard for your anticipation of the other side's requests. So, use your creativity. Write down a number of alternative ways in which you can fulfill your landlord's needs. One such list might include:

- Will pay rent immediately for longer lease
- Or will take longer lease for lower rent
- Will sign a "no noise" clause
- Will inventory apartment before entering and upon leaving for security damages
- Will pay bigger security deposit, but over a number of months
- Will offer to paint apartment for lower rent/do repairs for lower rent

These options will now be available to you as you negotiate with the landlord.

Does a negotiating plan guarantee success? No. Does it help you in a negotiation? Yes. A negotiating plan helps you think about all the parts of the deal that you can negotiate. For example, you may not care at all about a "no pets" clause, but now that you think the landlord will want one, you can ask him to give you something in return for that clause. Without your negotiating plan, you might not have realized that you had that bargaining chip when you first sat down to think about your negotiation.

It would be tempting to say that there is no risk involved in negotiating, but there's always a certain amount of danger lurking. The tendency to decide things impulsively is like a land mine waiting quietly for you to step on it. Feeling the pressure to close a deal without regard to how the terms affect you and your position is another one. To avoid these land mines, you have to do one last thing with your negotiating plan. The last thing you should do is write down fixed terms beyond which you cannot afford or allow yourself to go. Be serious and honest about these. Stick to them. If you know you cannot afford an apartment for more than $860 per month, you need to know that *before* you begin discussions. These bottom lines are your trip wires. If you ever see yourself about to sign an agreement that is below a trip wire, slow down and think hard. Use those trip wires to alert you that perhaps, in this case, no deal is the best deal.

4 The Proliferating Tip

Identification
You've got a deal basically agreed upon. The other side comes back and asks for something small, an insignificant thing that it would be silly to stop the deal over. Then they ask for another. And another. These are the tips you pay to get the deal done.

Note
The tips you pay in this situation are more annoying than substantive. But, over the long term, they can really eat away at your level of gratification. Please note that this tip doesn't mean anything large or deal-breaking thrust on you at the end of a negotiation. A tip is a small thing, something no one would balk over.

Solution
Have a tip list of your own ready. Every time they ask for one thing, offer to give it to them if they give you something on your list in return. Over time, they'll get tired of pestering you for tips—particularly if these tips are costing them more than they are getting.

If the landlord offers you an option you haven't considered, never agree to it immediately. As you'll see in chapter 6, split-second decisions tend to work against you. Ask for some time to think it over. Make another list. Try to identify the need that this new option satisfies. If you can find a more attractive alternative, offer it to the other person. If you can't find a better way and it seems fair, think about it one more time. Think about how it may affect your enjoyment of the agreement. For example, the landlord may propose a simple clause that reads, "Late payment of rent may result in eviction from the apartment." While you may plan on paying the rent on time every month, and you may have no problem with the idea behind that clause, you may want the landlord to spell out what she means by "late" payment and when the landlord would choose to exercise her "may result" option.

A good example of getting into the other side's head occurred during the February 15, 1995 NFL expansion draft. The Jacksonville Jaguars and the Carolina Panthers were two new teams entering the NFL. They were allowed by league rules to hold a draft of unprotected players from the teams already in the National Football League. The Jaguars chose first, with each team alternating picks. The Jaguars and the Panthers each made lists ranking the available players by ability, attitude, and experience, and assigned a value to each player. Then, the teams each made another list based on their best interpretation of the other side's valuation of those players. By making a list and assigning value from the point of view of the other side, both Jacksonville and Carolina were able to anticipate what players would be available when it came their turn to pick.

By anticipating the other side's needs and creating a negotiation plan, you'll be better prepared for most situations you'll encounter. You'll feel more relaxed and confident. The negotiation plan should guide you through, but should not be your only option for how to proceed. Negotiating without flexibility limits your ability to come to good terms for both sides.

What if the person negotiating is not the party involved on the other side? This happens all the time. If you've ever negotiated with a salesperson or an agent, you've been involved in this type of a negotiation. Always pay attention to the person you are negotiating with, not the corporation he works for. For example, Galaxo Products might be an international conglomerate with 1.2 billion in sales and outlets in 40,000 cities across the world, but the guy you are sitting across from, Sam Salesperson, has concerns far different than Galaxo Products does. Is he paid by commission? Is doing a greater volume of business more important to him than getting a better price? Is he under pressure because he hasn't closed a deal in months? Is he planning to leave the company and wants to keep a good relationship with your company in case a job opens up? In some ways, you are better off negotiating with a person who doesn't have something personal at stake, who doesn't feel the need to get the most out of *every* aspect of a negotiation. The important thing is to face your negotiator and understand his motivations.

Negotiating with the owner of a small business is usually more detail-oriented, more flexible, and more creative than negotiating with a corporation. The deal will be tougher to forge but it's more likely that a positive one will be found for both parties. Can you offer to take all of IBM to a baseball game to meet them? No, but with a smaller company it's a possibility.

5 The Staller

Identification
You make a request for a change in the terms of a deal. The negotiator for the other side says she has no problem with this, but she has to check with her boss. A day passes. Two days pass. You call back and the other party says there's no problem; it just takes time to get changes approved. Eventually, because it takes so long to get any change approved, you stop asking for anything more.

Note
Making concessions but stalling them seems arduous and onerous, but it's a time-honored technique of negotiating. Although it doesn't destroy good will, it can make you less eager to negotiate with that person again. It also involves very little conflict. If you can afford to stall a little bit, it's a useful technique because it discourages extra requests, but don't become a perpetual staller.

Solution
Whenever you make a request the other side agrees to, make sure you set a time that the change will be approved by. Like all terms, that time is negotiable. Pointing out a missed deadline to the other party allows you to bring to light their stalling tactics. Also, you can defuse the stalling tactic by not getting frustrated and simply continuing to address problems as they arise.

Negotiating Workshop #2

Preparing a Negotiating Plan

Read the following summary of positions and write down a negotiating plan for each side.

The Morristown Ice Show is negotiating with its two star ice dancers, Cathy Freeze and Doug Jardine. They are engaged to be married. The show has Cathy skating three solo routines, Doug skating one solo routine, and both skating the closing routine together. The closing routine has been hailed in the press as "the most romantic moment since Rhett swept Scarlett up the staircase in Gone With The Wind.*" The owner of the ice show, Drake Blane, gave each of them a chance when they were young and unknown. Since then, the ice show has grown in fame and prestige. They play to a packed house nearly every night. Drake worries that if Cathy and Doug leave the show, fewer people will come. He knows, however, that there are a limited number of ice shows in the country and none of the other shows need a feature act right now. But if the show shuts down for five days or more, Drake begins to run into money problems. After five days, he'll have to begin laying people off. After nine days, he'll have to stop paying people altogether. Cathy and Doug, while aware of some of Drake's financial pressures, don't know the whole story. Cathy has had an ankle problem in the past, which has sidelined her for a number of shows. In spite of the pain, she has performed whenever physically possible. Doug is also coming out with a book in the fall titled* My Life on the Ice—The Doug Jardine Story *and is booked to do a segment on "Oprah." Drake used to be a skater himself. He knows how hard the life is, but he is more committed to the ice show than to Cathy and Doug. Cathy and Doug each currently earn $300 per show. They are asking for five-year contracts at $1,000 per show each.*

Feeling Confident

By identifying your needs before you step into the room, you increase the likelihood that you will get more of what you want. Getting into the appropriate mindset before you enter the negotiating room will empower you and make it easier for you to attain your goals. It is easy to focus on all the pressures on you to make a deal work. It is more difficult to understand the pressures on the other party. And sometimes, it is most difficult to ask for more than you believe you can get. You feel that someone will be insulted, not take you seriously, or walk away. In these circumstances, you have to remember a few things.

Remember—you aren't negotiating alone. The other side is negotiating with you, because you have something they want.

Remember—you aren't the only one who can articulate needs. If the other side disagrees with your position, they have ample opportunity to bring it up.

Remember—all your initial work has prepared you for this moment. You have planned for most of the responses that can happen.

Remember—you know how to listen and react to what the other side says *and* what the other side means.

Remember—negotiation should create a positive, future-oriented relationship, not break up an existing one.

Remember—negotiation is more unpleasant for them than it is for you.

Remember—you now know how to negotiate well.

Negotiating Workshop #3

Preparation Checklist Test

Babs McClure and Gabby Donaldson are sitting across a table from each other. Gabby has arranged a meeting with Babs in order to procure Babs's pet wolverine, Mr. Rogers. Mr. Rogers has been Babs's pet for years, but she has made it known that for the right price, she'd be willing to part with him. In truth, Babs's arthritis has gotten bad and she cannot care for Mr. Rogers as well as she would like. Babs also knows that as Mr. Rogers has aged, his behavior has become increasingly erratic and, while posing no immediate danger, has made her quite nervous and reduced her quality of life. Gabby, on the other hand, has a set of triplets who have seen Mr. Rogers on a number of occasions and have fallen in love with him. Babs has prepared a negotiating plan about Gabby that looks as follows:

- Wants to buy my pet wolverine
- Wants to pay under $600
- Doesn't want to pay for shots
- Doesn't want to buy leash or collar or protective gloves
- Doesn't want to pay for additional health care costs for his kids
- Has kids waiting at home for "big surprise" daddy promised
- Wants to extend payment over time

Will probably ask:

- To buy wolverine
- $200 today, $100/month for three months
- I pay for shots
- I throw in gear
- To take wolverine home today (his kids' birthday)
- To get some kind of "Good Wolverine" guarantee so if Mr. Rogers bites or mauls one of his children, I will cover the cost

Will offer back to him:

- To sell him wolverine
- He can pay either $200 today, then $100 per month/
  four months
- Or $300 today, $200 one month from now, $100 one
  month after that
- To pay for shots (Mr. Rogers is already fully vaccinated)
- Gear for $50 more (less than half of retail)
- To give him Mr. Rogers today
- No guarantee, because I don't know how the kids will
  treat him

Gabby, who has read this book as well, has formulated his own
negotiating plan concerning Babs:

- She'll want $900 for wolverine
- She'll want to keep Mr. Rogers through the holidays
- Once she sells him, she won't want to pay for shots
  or anything
- She'll want full price for the gear
- She'll want the money up front

She'll ask for:

- $1,000 for the wolverine
- Sale in two weeks
- Wolverine as is
- $100 for the leash, collar and protective gloves

I will be creative and offer:

- $300 today for the wolverine, $400 three months from
  now
- $50 for the gear
- I'll take care of shots
- I get him today

- She gets unlimited visiting rights
- We'll bring him by once a week for a visit, if she doesn't want to travel
- Must deal today, though, or no deal

Answer the following questions about the negotiation that's about to ensue:

1. Who do you think is in a stronger bargaining position?
2. Do you think they will reach an agreement?
3. At what price do you think this agreement will be reached?
4. On what other terms do you think this agreement will be reached?
5. What other creative alternatives do you think could be offered by either party?
6. On a scale of 1-9, where 1 is no preparation and 9 is complete preparation, how prepared to you think Gabby is? And Babs?
7. What is the most important issue Gabby is not aware of?
8. What is the most important issue Babs is not aware of?

(Please note that the domestication and the incarceration of a free-born wolverine is not only cruel to the animal and against federal law, but also enormously dangerous. Pound for pound, the wolverine is the most fierce animal on the face of the earth. Wolverines have been known to hold at bay packs of thirty similarly sized predators at the same time. So in other words, don't do this at home. If you ever find yourself negotiating this deal, the best deal is definitely no deal.)

CHAPTER 3

Communication

So you're in the room, and you're prepared—you have information about the other side, you have information about the other negotiator, and you've prepared a plan. You have everything written down, you have anticipated most of the possible directions the discussion can go in, and you feel in control of the negotiation. As the other person walks in, you begin to talk about all the reasons your deal is better than their deal, and why they must make concessions on a number of points. But they don't agree with you. And what's more, they take offense at what you're saying. You still just don't understand their argument. There are words. They thank you for your time, and then they leave. You are left with a pad full of information and no deal at all.

Many negotiations fail not because a good deal didn't exist somewhere for both parties. They fail because the parties couldn't clearly communicate their needs and wants to each other. Negotiations that fail because of communication breakdowns almost always could have been successful.

There is a myth that negotiations start when the two parties begin to discuss the terms of a given deal. This myth involves two people who don't know each other, talk about nothing but the deal at hand, and then part. The myth also holds that the two negotiators have their own independent sets of concerns and will work within a mutually beneficial framework to get the best deal, but that nothing else will influence the outcome of the negotiation.

Actually, most negotiations occur in continuing relationships. Contracts, supplier deals, product support, even car purchases—all of these can be considered ongoing relationships. If you feel that

6

First Draft

Identification
You come to terms on a deal, and the other side offers to put them into a contract for the next session. When you receive the contract, there are terms in there that clearly favor the side drafting the contract. You request that the offending terms be removed, but the other party asks for concessions to make up for them.

Note
There is an advantage to writing the first draft of any contract when it's possible. You shouldn't change anything that has been clearly agreed upon, for example price or terms of payment, but anything that hasn't been settled on can be put in to your advantage.

Solution
If you have the option, create the first draft of any contractual agreement yourself. If the other side presents you with a drawn-up contract before you've given the go-ahead, tell them that you too have drafted a contract (or will do so shortly) and you'd like to compare the two point by point.

the dealership provided you with little support when the car broke down, or that they sold you a complete lemon, then you'll never buy another car from them. You won't recommend to your friends that they buy a car from that dealership, and in fact you'll steer people away if they ask you. Car dealers have an interest in behaving fairly and maintaining a relationship with you. The one-shot "get as much as you can" method of bargaining isn't as useful as you might imagine. Negotiators are people, and deals are best treated like good relationships—with the long term in mind.

Negotiation begins when you first meet the other party. You shake hands and introduce yourselves. At this point, you're both sizing each other up and, if possible, establishing a relationship. If you have an instinct to jump directly into the negotiation, don't. Connect first as a human being. Discuss interests, hobbies, or families with the other party. Don't even try to connect these topics to the negotiation. Try to find some common ground with the other person. Listen carefully to her description of herself. Establishing yourself as a careful listener will work to your advantage in the negotiation.

If you have the good fortune to meet with the negotiator before you're actually negotiating you can find out more information in a non-confrontational way. Consider this scenario. A bond broker for Merrill Lynch, a full-service brokerage firm, went out for dinner with a group that included a salesperson for another firm. During the course of the dinner, the salesperson got to talking about his job. He mentioned that his bonus was coming up in two months, and that his company based it solely on volume of work, not on the dealer who got the best price. The next day, the bond broker and the salesperson were negotiating the price of a bond trade, and the salesperson asked for a better price. The broker responded with a lower price but twice the volume. The salesperson hesitated but took the trade. By finding out what was important for the salesperson, the broker found a way to improve his own position while fulfilling the needs of the salesperson. Casual talk and friendly discussions can provide you with powerful tools for a future negotiation.

This initial contact is known as pre-communication. As negotiators, you will find ample time to disagree, discuss and comment on the deals you propose to each other. By pre-communicating, you are, in effect, preparing for the negotiation. The simple act of looking at someone's family photos, for example, establishes a connection between you that makes further communication easier.

Once you've pre-communicated with the other party, you still must be careful to send appropriate signals. Sometimes what you say is less important than how you say it.

"You know I like your house, Donny, but the eaves are falling apart, the gutters need work, I'd have to paint the whole thing..."

"Quit with the song and dance, Jerry. It's $40,000. Do you want to buy it or not?"

"I'll give you $15,000 for it. You've worn this house into the ground with your parties."

"What? Is that a joke?"

"It's the best offer you'll get for this dump. I'm doing you a favor with this offer."

"Don't do me any favors."

"Don't be a jerk."

"Who's the jerk, jerk?"

"Don't you call me a jerk. I'll give you $10,000 for this garbage pile you and your illiterate stinking kids live in."

(They scuffle.)

Not all negotiations go this poorly, but some do, and even some that appear to go better still have the same basic problem: communication. Jerry has reservations about the condition of the house. Donny is interested in getting a good price for his house. Ideally, they would both express their desires in a way that keeps the negotiation moving. Obviously, neither did.

Keeping your verbal communication focused on the negotiating situation, not on the person negotiating, is an important communication skill. You want to have plenty of information about the person you are negotiating with so that you are well-prepared, but when you sit down to negotiate a deal, both parties should focus on the strengths, weaknesses, and terms of the negotiation—not each other. Here's another possible way the above negotiation could have gone:

"Donny, this is one fine house."

"Sure Jerry, we've lived here for twenty years, and we've loved every minute of it. If you have $40,000, it's all yours."

"Have you had any chance to check the eaves?"

"Yeah, I've been meaning to fix those up."

"Did you paint the house in the last few years?"

"Actually, no. We haven't painted in about ten years."

"Because if I buy this place, I'm going to want to fix a few things up. Also, after twenty years, the gutters probably need replacing—you know, just part of the normal wear and tear. Those storms last year ruined my gutters."

"Yeah, those storms were awful, weren't they?"

"With all the things I want to do to it, I just can't pay $40,000 for the house. You've got a great one here, and I'd love to have it, but I really can only spend about $20,000 and still put the house in the shape that me and my family want. You see my problem?"

"I do, Jerry, I do. And I understand that all these little things puts you in a tough financial position. I'll tell you what—I'll take care of the eaves and the gutters, and I'll come down on price. But if I'm going to do these things for you, I can't take less than $30,000. At that price, you're getting a great house in great shape at a great price."

"I'll go home and talk about it with my family, but I think you're being fair and honest. Thanks for showing me a way we might get this done."

"A pleasure negotiating with you, Jerry."

The tone of this negotiation is much more positive, and this one has a greater likelihood of reaching an agreement. By focusing on the house rather than on the person, on the problem rather than on the history with the negotiator, Jerry and Donny are able to work together to form an arrangement. Jerry states his concerns in a non-judgmental, objective fashion—giving Donny the leeway to step in and offer suggestions or solutions. Finding ways to phrase objections and reservations in a clear, positive, and forward-thinking manner is the hallmark of an excellent dealmaker.

It's important to note something that is all too prevalent in negotiations but never should be: personal feelings and emotions. When you negotiate on the basis of emotion, you follow a path that leads nowhere. This does not mean that you should not express yourself at all in a negotiation. Sometimes, a well-placed laugh at a particular offer or an expression of outrage is warranted by the situation. Just remember that your emotions should work for you, not against you. Personal differences can be settled at a later date and in a different manner. Don't try to get even with someone for a personal slight in a professional forum. It can only come back to haunt you.

Many people think they sound more informed and professional if they can bandy about a few polysyllabic words to impress the other side. In reality, a good communicator uses the simplest, most honest, and most direct vocabulary possible.

Bad Vocabulary
"I've undergone a rigorous statistical analysis of those datum provided by your party."
"Pecuniary matters are secondary to issues of mechanical exactitude."
"Salutations and well met, noble adversary."

Better Vocabulary
"I've looked at your numbers."
"I don't care about cost—I just want it to work."
"Hi."

How do you communicate bad news? Directly and as soon as you know that you have bad news to communicate. If a deal is unmakable on certain terms, state that right away. If you receive information that a deal you have negotiated has been rejected by someone else—your boss, say, or your family—communicate that immediately. People don't like bad news, but they like being deceived even less. If you send signals that you are willing to do something you have no intention of doing, the other party will feel cheated and angry when you reveal that you will not do it. Negotiating on the basis of false promises only leads to a loss of your credibility and to ill will.

7 The Beggar

Identification
A negotiation keeps turning to the subject of the other party's problems. You hear how he is really having trouble at his company, and how badly he needs your business. He promises that the next time you negotiate, he'll give you a break if you give him one now.

Note
Promises are easy. Performance is difficult. This kind of negotiating tactic takes the deal away from the professional arena. This tactic loses more often than it wins.

Solution
Tell the other side that unless they want to negotiate two deals at once, including the future one where they make major concessions, you're not interested. It may seem hardhearted, but negotiating is a professional skill. Negotiators have to behave professionally, period.

Body Language

As a baby, you first learn to interact with others by giving and receiving simple verbal and visual commands. You're hungry—you cry. Eventually, someone figures out that you're hungry and feeds you. When you do something good, they smile. When you've had enough Cheerios, you throw the bowl on the floor. Those are the basics. You pick up clues on how to get people around you to react and respond.

So why don't you continue these methods as an adult? You've learned more complicated methods of communication—words, signs, symbols—and you feel that those methods more effectively communicate your wants and needs to other people. You communicate using the most advanced tools you have at your disposal. If you had a hammer lying next to you, you wouldn't pound nails using a rock. You'd use the hammer. You'd be silly to do otherwise. But when people are trying to keep their reactions hidden, you have to go back to your childhood training and interpret not only what they say, but what they do as well.

We're not asking you to abandon your advanced tools of communication—but we are asking you to notice the body language of the other party and to pay attention to the physical communication that goes on during a negotiation. In many ways, it can be the most meaningful communication you and the other side share.

Someone's posture, reactions, and body language let you know a lot about her beliefs and intentions. For example, if you are selling your used lawnmower, and you name a price of $120 to a prospective buyer who says, "No, I can't do that," but takes out his wallet and keeps stroking the smooth handle of your bright red mower, well, you just might want to keep that price high. Through his actions, he is telling you that he wants your lawnmower, and that he's willing to pay a fair price for it. Now, while you're getting important information from someone's reaction, keep in mind that communication takes place in two directions. How you sit, react, respond, and move all communicate to the other side your intentions. Be aware of what you do, as well as what the other side does. Involuntarily, you may be giving the other side information you wanted to keep private.

What do you do when other people overreact to every statement or word you utter? You have a few options that we'll explore in chapter 7, which is about the deal itself. At this point, it is enough to recognize that your physical reactions, and the reactions of your opponents, are reasonable weathervanes in determining the direction of any negotiation. Sometimes, by identifying the distracting behavior and bringing it out in the open, you can spur a quick improvement in your negotiating partner's attitude.

> *Sometimes a tactic will take you by surprise, but that's no reason to panic. "One job interview I went on was very strange," said one attorney at the firm of Parker, Durhee, Rosoff and Haft. "I sat in a seat opposite the interviewer, and he began by speaking in this barely audible voice. 'Now, this job is about working hard...' He barely made any noise! I answered his questions in the same whispered tones. 'Well, I feel I'm quite qualified...' By the end of the interview, we both were speaking in normal tones. Don't let anyone intimidate you. I got the job, by the way."*

While there are an infinite variety of human responses and reactions, they can be grouped into the following basic categories:

1. Negative Reactions

If you've ever said something you've regretted, you know that it is often easier to tell when someone is disappointed, angry, or offended than when they are pleased. Negative reactions are easily identifiable: blinking, squirming, wincing, flinching, sighing, yelling, cursing, crying, or banging around furniture. Keep your eye out not just for flying chairs but for more subtle signs of discomfort to tell you that you've said something displeasing.

2. Positive Reactions

While excitement can be more difficult to spot, it's important to recognize when you've said or touched upon something that the other person is psyched about. Once you know someone is interested in a certain topic or idea, you can use that knowledge to your best advantage. When people react positively, they tend to do things like lean forward, take notes, come back to a topic when you've moved on, focus more intently when the subject is mentioned, or simply smile. But be careful—a positive reaction may mean you've offered the other side something too appealing. Maybe you could easily have offered less.

3. No Reaction

Sometimes people don't show any visible signs of emotion or reaction to anything you say. These people are difficult, if not impossible, to read. You may be tempted to adopt this stonewall approach, but don't fall into the false sense of powers it offers. We don't believe that offering no reaction at all is the best way to negotiate. The more clues you can offer and the more unwavering you can make your position, the fewer problems due to miscommunication you will ultimately have. People who evince no reaction are usually under the impression that if they admit they are human, you may gain some advantage over them. In fact, allowing a connection to develop by offering direct clues about your responses has a variety of positive effects on any negotiation. People are more willing to educate (see chapter 4) and explain things to those whom they feel a connection with. So, while there are important times when remaining silent can enhance your position (see chapter 7), in general, keeping your reactions honest and aboveboard is the most fruitful technique.

> *"I'll give you $400 for your golf clubs, bag included."*
>
> *(No response)*
>
> *"What, you want more?"*
>
> *"I'm thinking about it."*
>
> *"Well, give me an answer."*
>
> *(No response)*
>
> *"Look, I've got another meeting at six. What do you think about the price."*
>
> *(Silence)*
>
> *"O.K. We don't have a deal. Now get out of my office."*
>
> *(No response)*
>
> *"I'm going to call security if you don't leave. Now."*
>
> *(No response)*
>
> *"I'm calling security. I'm serious."*
>
> *(No response)*
>
> *"Well, at least lock up when you leave."*

When people think of communication, they usually think of what they say and what they do. While this is part of communication, it's often not the most important part. The most important part of communication is usually listening. Not just looking like you're listening or acting like you're listening, not thinking about what you're going to have for dinner while nodding at the other person, but carefully listening to her with your full attention. What is she saying? What is she trying to tell you? What is she communicating to you?

Read Herman Melville's great story "Bartleby the Scrivener." *This funny and eerie story involves a negotiation that goes absolutely nowhere.*

Listening attentively has two positive effects on negotiation. First, you gain valuable information about the position of the other side. By listening carefully, you can hear not only the actual requests the other side makes, but the needs that lie behind the requests. If you then have creative alternatives prepared for them, they are going to be more willing to consider them. The second positive effect is that the other side feels they are being taken seriously. When the other side feels they are truly being listened to, they are more likely to afford you serious consideration when your time to speak comes.

Imagine you are in an English class and you feel the professor is treating you unfairly. You report this to the dean of the college. The dean is talking on the telephone as you relate your story. When you finish, she sends you out of her office. Two weeks later, you receive a letter saying that the professor's behavior has been upheld by the university. Now, do you feel that you have been fairly heard?

Imagine the same situation. You have the same meeting with the dean. She listens carefully to your story. She takes notes. She tells you what to expect—that she will meet with the professor, she will meet with other students in the class, and that she will inform you of any action taken by the university in two weeks. In one week, she calls you to explain that she has finished investigating your allegations, and expects to rule this week. She asks you if you have anything to add. One week later, the dean calls you to explain that she is going to uphold the professor's position. She refers to your own grievance, and to comments the professor made, and to information received from other students in the class. She explains the decision and gives you her office number in case there are any incidents in which you feel you are treated unfairly in the future. Later that week, you receive a letter confirming your conversation with the dean.

Which scenario do you think better encourages a long-term relationship, the first or the second? Surely, the second scenario leaves the student feeling more satisfied. Even though the same result emerges in each case, the student is clearly going to be more gratified by the attention and the care that the dean took in the second scenario. The lesson from this example is simple. By listening carefully, you do something important for your negotiation: You establish a base of respect and communication that helps you achieve a fulfilling, fair agreement that fosters a long-term relationship.

8 Side-Issuers

Identification
The other party wants to focus on side issues exclusively. They give way on every minor point before the discussion reaches the main point. Then, when you reach the main subject, the other side keeps directing you to all the concessions that they made earlier. As a result, you find it difficult to reach an agreement on the main issue of the negotiation.

Note
Side-issuing is not recommended for a couple of reasons. First, each issue in a deal should be decided in conjunction with the other issues. Without looking at the deal as a whole, any single issue is unimportant. Second, side-issuing is easily defeated. While it is sometimes helpful to begin with issues that aren't the central one, the main issue will have to be dealt with at some point regardless.

Solution
There are two ways to defuse this. You can get the other side to agree at the outset to negotiate the contract in its entirety, not point by point. This gives you a look at all of the deal and allows you to decide what it means to you as a whole before any one term is made final. You can also offer to trade some of your minor concessions for one major one when the other side gets to the main issue. If the other side wants to give you more bargaining chips to play with, by all means, let them.

Two recent baseball negotiations failed because one side didn't listen carefully and take into account emotions. During the 1993 baseball off-season, Greg Maddux and Barry Bonds were both aggressively pursued by the New York Yankees. One of the most profitable teams in the major leagues, the Yankees were able to offer the most money to each agent, but they lost both players. Initially they pursued Maddux. They brought him to New York, took him to see a show, let him answer questions to the press, and offered him thirty million dollars over seven years. When his agent seemed hesitant to commit to the deal, the Yankees offered him thirty-four million dollars for seven years.

What the Yankees didn't know was that Greg Maddux wanted a quiet, suburban life. Whenever Maddux had been in town to play against a New York team, he had stayed in his hotel room and played video games, slightly overwhelmed and turned off by the whole city scene. The difference between thirty and thirty-four million dollars didn't mean that much to him. The quality of life that New York offered him and his children did. Had the Yankees shown him the suburban New York area more thoroughly, they would have had a much better chance of signing him. Paying attention to Maddux's past emotional reaction to being in New York would have helped the Yankees make their offer appealing to him.

Barry Bonds was the premier left-handed hitter available in the 1993 free-agent market. All the signs seemed to be in favor of Bonds's signing with the Yankees. Yankee stadium favors left-handed hitters. His best friend, Bobby Bonilla, played for the rival New York team, the Mets. Bonds's father had been a Yankee. The Yankees believed that all that needed to be discussed was money, so that's all they discussed. They offered him forty-three million dollars for seven years. His agent inquired about an eighth year. The Yankees said, "Alright. How about forty-three million dollars for eight years." This response did nothing but aggravate Barry Bonds. He accepted a lower offer by the San Francisco Giants who also offered his father, Bobby, a job as a coach. The San Francisco Giants also made Barry Bonds the feature player on their team, a promise that wasn't forthcoming from the Yankees.

By being insensitive to Barry Bonds in two ways, first in neglecting to listen to his needs, second in responding to his concerns in a cavalier way, the Yankees lost him. Had the Yankees been more attentive to the concerns voiced by the other side, perhaps Barry Bonds would be in pinstripes today.

NEGOTIATING WORKSHOP #4

Communication Skills Exercise

Each of the following questions has an answer that is best in terms of communication, tone, and attitude. Choose the best answer for each question.

1. For three years, Silly Plastic has been the largest client of McGuffy advertising, where you are an account executive. Over that time, Silly Plastic has increased its market share, and is now the industry leader. Silly Plastic now wants to reduce the cost of the advertising contract but keep the obligations the same. A Silly Plastic executive says, "We think that your costs are too high, and now that we're at the top of our industry, we'd be a prize possession for any advertising firm. How much lower can your price go?" Your best response is:

   (A) "Costs are only one part of a relationship. You're not looking at the whole package. Take a look at everything we do for you. I'm sure you'll be satisfied."
   (B) "I'd rather not discuss this now. When our contract expires, we'll discuss anything you want."
   (C) "Much, much lower. Whatever you say, sir."
   (D) "We can talk about any terms you find improper. Your account is important to us, and we'll do our best to find a fair and reasonable solution."
   (E) "How dare you ask us to reduce our price! After all we've done for you!"

2. Every time you mention a certain cost increase on a particular product, the person who is negotiating for the other side winces visibly, as if in pain. He has done this nine or ten times during the discussion. A good response might be:
   (A) "This cost increase seems to bother you. Let's talk about it and, if I can, I'd like to explain to you the better product you're getting for your money."
   (B) "Look. This wincing business has to stop."
   (C) "I understand that you are having trouble with these price increases, but if we are going to get through this negotiation, you have to behave a little more maturely."
   (D) "Get used to the new prices. I'm not budging on price, even though it upsets you."
   (E) "I understand and feel your pain. We all hate price increases, and I'm truly truly sorry to be the bearer of bad news. If you want, we could stall the negotiations and have a nice double mocha espresso while we explore these feelings and see where they lead us."

3. Upon beginning a negotiation, a good first step would be:
   (A) to ask the other side if they have any questions.
   (B) to remain silent until the other side has stated their position.
   (C) to shake hands.
   (D) to inform them of competitive offers you have received.
   (E) to give them a brief history of your company.

4. You've made your best offer to the other side, and they have rejected it. You've informed them that this was your best offer. You've offered to negotiate other parts of the deal to find some way to make the deal work, and they have declined. They've come to you with an offer they say is their best offer, but it is in no way acceptable to you. At this point, the most reasonable response would be:
   (A) imploring the other side to return to the negotiating table.
   (B) a handshake and an offer of a chance to work together in the future.
   (C) accepting their deal.
   (D) offering to split the difference between the two offers.
   (E) offering a third party to come in and decide the negotiation for both parties.

5. An important communication tool for any negotiation is:
   (A) attire
   (B) listening
   (C) a modem
   (D) information
   (E) education

6. When negotiating, you should pay attention to:
   (A) the other side's spoken communication.
   (B) the other side's physical communication.
   (C) your own physical communication.
   (D) your own reactions to their offers.
   (E) all of the above.

7. When meeting the other negotiator outside the negotiating process, you should:
   (A) discuss the terms of the negotiation.
   (B) review the scope of the negotiation.
   (C) offer a creative, new solution to the negotiation.
   (D) discuss anything but the negotiation.
   (E) brainstorm for new, creative alternatives for the negotiation.

8. One a scale of 1 to 10, where 10 is the most important and 1 is the least important, how would you rank communication among negotiating skills?
   (A) 1-3
   (B) 4-5
   (C) 5-6
   (D) 6-7
   (E) 8-10

9. You are the buyer for an auto supply shop. You have a relationship with a parts supplier who has consistently given you the best parts at the best price. They have been responsive to your requests and to all your needs over the years. You learn, from a piece of confidential information, that they need to sign you to a long-term contract desperately, at pretty much any cost. The appropriate action for you to take would be:

   (A) to tell them of your knowledge and assure them you will not exceed the bounds of fairness.
   (B) to listen to their offer without revealing your knowledge.
   (C) to demand to renegotiate all contracts with the supply firm now, telling them you know of their position.
   (D) to arrange a different time to negotiate the contract, because they would be under unfair duress.
   (E) to offer to help out with their crisis in any way you can.

10. The person negotiating for the other side is obnoxious, loud, and abusive to his subordinates. You are personally offended by his behavior, but within the negotiation his actions have been professional. A good way to handle this situation is to:

    (A) bring attention to his obnoxious behavior and ask if he would please be more considerate to his personnel.
    (B) behave in exactly the same way he acts, providing him with a mirror reflecting his own behavior back to him.
    (C) ignore it until it affects the negotiation.
    (D) stall the negotiation with an ultimatum: either he behaves civilly and issues an apology to his subordinates or you won't negotiate.
    (E) take him aside at some point and offer him tips on how to improve his interpersonal skills.

CHAPTER 4

Strategic Education

"The reason I called this meeting was to tell you that unless you lower your price, we're going to have to go to another supplier."

"But we've been doing business for twenty years! Has our product's quality declined?"

"No, not at all. We've always been pleased with your service and your product."

"Then what are you unhappy with?"

"Your price."

"But we can't go any lower! We're not making that much money on your order as it is."

"I have a lower offer on a similar product."

"What did they offer?"

"Considerably lower."

"I don't believe it."

"Believe it."

"I'll have to get back to you."

In any negotiation, information is power. The more information you have, the more you are able to anticipate your negotiating partner's needs to your own advantage. Yet there are times when sharing information with the other side is the most beneficial thing you can do. Many negotiations go nowhere, because people don't understand others' need and concerns. Where there is a true lack of understanding, offering some well-considered information can break a deadlock and encourage communication. The process of informing the other party without undermining your own position is called Strategic Education. Imagine the above negotiation with the following educational information brought into play.

"The reason I called this meeting was to tell you that unless you lower your price, we're going to have to go to another supplier."

"But we've been doing business for twenty years! Has our product's quality declined?"

"No, not at all. We've always been pleased with your service and your product."

"Then what are you unhappy with?"

"Your price."

"Are you tied to your design? You know, you have ordered a custom paperweight."

"What do you mean?"

"The normal size for our paperweight is two inches by two inches. The one you've asked for is three inches by three inches."

"We don't really care about the size. We just used the same specifications we've always used."

"Oh? If you don't mind adjusting the size, you can save some money."

"We never knew."

"Also, if you don't want the fancy raised corporate seal, you can save some money there."

"Really?"

"And, if you decide to order in bulk, I can get you a further discount. It's the initial mold that costs money to produce. Duplicates get cheaper after we make the first one."

"And all of these things will lead to lower prices?"

"Absolutely."

"I'm glad we had this discussion."

"So am I. I'll get you estimates on what the new models will cost as soon as I can. If you have any questions, feel free to give me a call."

By educating his client about the manufacturing process, this agent lets both parties work together toward a common goal—a good, long-term, mutually beneficial relationship. Strategic Education should be used to assure a person that he is getting the best value for his price. Here's an example: In 1994, Brooklyn Heights, New York became a neighborhood with nearly full occupancy for one- and two-bedroom apartments. Brokers, who were used to showing their clients six or seven satisfactory apartments, were squeezed into showing their clients only one or two that fit their criteria. Clients began to express dissatisfaction with individual brokers, accusing them of not having access to the good apartments. The brokers got together and assembled a fact sheet about average occupancy in Brooklyn Heights, average rent in Brooklyn Heights, and the number of apartments available in Brooklyn Heights by month. They printed it up on stationery from the "Brooklyn Heights Brokers Association" and distributed it to all their clients. Almost immediately, client satisfaction rose by eighty-five percent! This use of Strategic Information won over the client base without eroding the position of the brokers at all.

9

Fact or Fiction?

Identification
The other side presents you with a number of facts you know to be incorrect or claims that a set of facts doesn't exist that you know does exist.

Note
You should never use this ploy. This is the quickest way to move your deal from the realm of negotiation to the realm of litigation. As in lawsuit. As in bad news.

Solution
Ask questions that reveal your knowledge and give the other side a chance to change their earlier statements. A simple "are those mileage figures for the city, too, and is that based on having four people in the car or fewer?" can give the other side a chance to correct their inaccuracies. If they continue to misrepresent themselves, state the facts that you believe to be true and walk away if they continue to lie. Anyone who can't be trusted during the negotiation can't be trusted to perform in a business relationship.

What percentage of American communities rely totally on trucks for surface freight transportation?

☐ 10% ☐ 67% ☐ 27% ☐ 50%

Two out of three, or 67% of American communities are totally dependent on truck transportation for virtually all their freight service. Truck service is a vital factor to your quality of life.

What's the average time for a truck to deliver Florida oranges to a Midwest grocery store?

☐ 70 hours ☐ 4 days ☐ 38 hours

Thirty-eight hours. Refrigerated trucks make it possible for consumers to enjoy fresh fruit and vegetables all year round.

How many miles has truck driver N. F. Plunkett, Jr. driven without a single accident?

☐ 800,000 ☐ 1,200,000 ☐ 2,500,000

In his 37 years on the road, Plunkett has logged more than two and one-half million miles with a spotless safety record. He has also been honored for his acts of good-will and heroism. That's why he earned the American Trucking Associations' highest award, the 1984 Driver of the Year. As the nation's best professional truck driver, Plunkett is one of thousands who practice safe driving on America's highways.

There's no question about it. The nation's freight transportation system is the finest in the world. And the trucking industry is a vital part of that system. That's why we're working to provide businesses with the economical, reliable, responsive service they require to stay competitive. And since we're all consumers, everyone benefits.

Trucks. The driving force behind American business.

ATA FOUNDATION

The American Trucking Associations Foundation, Inc
1616 P St. N.W., Washington, D.C. 20036

Strategic Education is standard operating procedure for most large organizations. Large lobbying industries put out their own "fact sheets," like the one above, that they send to political and industry leaders and the general public to strengthen their positions when issues affecting them are ultimately negotiated. The Dairy Lobby, the Truckers' Union, the AMA, and even the ABA regularly produce and disseminate statistics and information aimed at educating people about what they do, and what strictures they're working under. Whenever possible, you should use the process of Strategic Education to further your own negotiations. Use the following basic guidelines to determine when you should and when you should not educate—and remember, these are only rough guidelines. There's no substitute for your own considered judgment of a particular situation.

You should use Strategic Education when:

1. You are providing a service that is not necessarily visible or apparent.
2. You are providing assistance for a very complicated subject or deal.
3. You have information about external events that will affect the outcome and that will make your position appear rational or appropriate.
4. You are bargaining with someone who has no experience in the area of the deal.

Strategic Education doesn't have to be in the form of a written report or a long, detailed conversation. The goal is to give the other party the most clear picture of the process you are involved in without miring them in the details of your position. One good example of this is the free tours of its refinery in Northern California that Chevron provides for each of its shareholders. Chevron employees will take any shareholder on a tour of the refinery, not only showing them the enormous oil tanks, but also giving them a detailed lecture that explains the refining process. Shareholders are invited into the research and development labs and shown the glass-making facilities where Chevron makes its own glass equipment rather than purchasing expensive custom glass tools. This process shows shareholders that abstract numbers and quarterly reports reflect physical, tangible things. Shareholders are made to feel that they are not only investing in a company, they are participating in the company's future. Education, Chevron understands, works to everyone's advantage in promoting shareholder satisfaction.

Let's take another example. Say you run a hardware store and make a ten percent profit on every item. Someone walks into the store and asks you how much profit you make on every item. Do you tell him ten percent, opening up the opportunity for him to try to negotiate that percentage downward? Do you let him know your costs so he can determine your profit margin? Of course not.

The moral here is that there are times when educating your negotiating partner can work to your disadvantage. Educating when you shouldn't can actually undermine your position. You should offer information only when you are certain that it will work in your favor. But be judicious. This does not mean withholding information indiscriminately, especially if the other party is likely to discover that information eventually.

The editor of Columbia Magazine was being contacted repeatedly by a company that wanted to design and print the magazine's covers. Finally, the company was granted an interview. When the magazine stated its needs and the price they were currently paying, the design and printing firm looked defeated. Their price was higher. Undeterred, however, they kept asking questions about the magazine's specifications and print run and production costs, and then asked to arrange another meeting in a week. During that week, the design firm spoke with other printing firms, adjusted their own prices, and took new quotations on long-term supplies contracts. When they met again with the magazine the next week, they had put together a package for the entire production of the magazine that was lower priced and longer termed than the magazine's current production budget. They got the contract.

Remember that the other side can use the information you provide to find out more about what you do and what your costs are. If you offer too much detail, you can open yourself up to all kinds of potentially meddlesome requests. When you offer information on a large process, you may be needlessly alerting the other side to the position you intend to take during the negotiation. You may also end up steering them to people in your corporation who may inadvertently give away information. Strategic Education is only effective when used in the proper way at the appropriate time. When you try to use it too soon, in the wrong place, or inappropriately, it can be deadly to your position. The following scenario demonstrates the peril lurking in an attempt at Strategic Education.

"I'm not sure about the cost of this car. Tell me again how you got to this price?"

"Well lots of things go into this price. There's the special engineering, the unique materials we use, the custom color, the transportation expenses, the shipping costs, the overhead, the storage costs..."

"So if I get a non-custom color, would the price go down?"

"Well, sure, but..."

"And where does it get shipped in to?"

"It comes off the boat in California. Then it has to be driven on long, flatbed trucks across the country..."

"So if my cousin picks it up in California, I can save all those transportation and shipping expenses?"

"Well, it's a little more complicated than that..."

"And if you tell me when the shipments are coming in, I can avoid the storage costs also, right?"

"Those costs are sort of built into the price..."

"So you can't take them out, even if I don't use them?"

"Well, I'll have to talk to my manager..."

"Go ahead."

"What?"

"Talk to your manager. Actually, bring him over. I'd like to ask him about this stuff."

"I'd rather not involve him, so let's see if we can take care of this ourselves. I'll give you $200 off the price of the car."

"How'd you get that number?"

"Well, just trying to get you a better deal."

"Great. I'll take the $200 off. Then if I get a non-custom color, have my cousin pick it up in California, and you tell me the date the car arrives, I can get even more off. Let's talk to your manager about all the money you just saved me."

Do you think this buyer is going to get a better deal on this car? Absolutely. Do you think that the car salesperson is going to be praised by his manager for Strategic Education? Not a chance.

By educating his potential client about the specific costs included in the final price of the car, this car dealer has opened up each part of the price structure to negotiation. Note also that the car dealer revealed an aversion to referring things to his boss. The potential client can now use that to his advantage. When you reveal internal information or potential positions the other side wouldn't know about, trying to use Strategic Education can be counterproductive.

At times, it also may be a good idea to put the other side in the position of needing to offer *you* more information. When you let them try to educate you (even though you have solid information about the process and the product) you gain valuable insight into their position. Sometimes the smartest move you can make is to ask to be further enlightened. Let the other side talk and listen carefully.

10 | *Pressure Cookers*

Identification
You've come to negotiate and it seems the air is filled with tension. It's hot. The sun is in your eyes. They only take breaks every six hours. The entire situation has been designed to be as unpleasant as possible. They've created a veritable pressure cooker, trying to get you to feel so unpleasant that you want to conclude the negotiation as soon as possible.

Note
This tactic is only useful if the other party is a novice negotiator. Skilled or experienced negotiators will have encountered it before, and know many ways to defuse the situation.

Solution
As with many situations that are grossly unfair to one side, merely bringing the situation to light can help. If you say, "I'd love to negotiate this contract with you, but is there anywhere else we can negotiate? This room is unbearable. If there isn't any other place here, perhaps we could do it at my office. Or perhaps we should do this another day." Giving the other side a number of options makes them appear tyrannical if they say they want to continue the negotiation with the situation as it is.

NEGOTIATING WORKSHOP #5

Playing Dumb

Read the following negotiation discussion and write down the five potential negotiating gains that result from asking to be provided with more information.

"I'm not sure I understand what exactly it is that your company does or supplies. It's just me, I know that it's obvious to you, but if you could explain it, I'd really appreciate it."

"No problem. We produce office supplies in four different locations around the country. We produce paper, pencils, paper clips, rubber bands, folders, and typewriter ribbons. You buy your paper clips from us."

"Do all our offices across the country buy from you?"

"No. I think your branch is the only one that purchases from us."

"And here we only buy paper clips?"

"Yes. And I think our new paper clip will revolutionize your office."

"Do you make them near here?"

"Actually, the new ones are made in New Mexico."

"We have an office in New Mexico, you know."

"Fascinating. These new clips have twice the strength of the old clips and should last twice as long as the old ones, so it might cut your paper clip needs in half!"

"How long should these clips last?"

"Using normal wear and tear, around six years."

"Unbelievable."

"However, because they are so improved and so long-lasting, the price has gone up."

"By how much?"

"By only two cents per clip."

"How much did they cost before?"

"They're so improved, you can't really compare them with the old clips—"

"How much did they cost before?"

"Three cents per clip."

"Are you using different materials?"

"We've re-engineered the design to spread the stress more evenly throughout the clip itself."

"Are you using any different materials?"

"No, but the cost of raw materials has increased since last year."

"By how much?"

"That I can't tell you."

"By forty percent?"

"No, not that much, of course. But they have increased."

"I don't know much about the life of paper clips and the like. Do you have any studies that would show me about the lifespan of paper clips?"

"I'm sure we have something back at the office. I'll make a call."

"And if you could get me anything about the cost of your raw materials, it'd help me approach my bosses and explain your cost increases. Oh yeah, one more question. How long have we been doing business?"

"Ten years."

"And have your prices ever gone down?"

"I'm not sure. You know prices. They always go up."

"I see. Thanks for your time. If you can get me that information as soon as possible, I'll study it and call you if I have any further questions. It'd be a big help to me in reviewing this clip contract."

"I'll have it sent right over."

Once you've determined that some Strategic Education might help your negotiation, your next consideration is whether you want to be the party doing the educating. Some negotiations will be best helped by offering a third party to confirm facts you've already presented. We've all seen commercials that say "We'll beat any price!" Well, sometimes it makes sense to try them out. Show the store the better price. Let them call the store with the better price and see if they can deliver. Sometimes directing the other party to an uninvolved group can help verify your facts and prove that you are acting in good faith and presenting everything in a fair manner.

Think of how a good doctor will make a major diagnosis. It is common practice for doctors to suggest you get a second opinion to confirm or reject the initial diagnosis. In this way, a doctor gains credibility. Any outside reference point can be useful when you're negotiating. It ensures that the results will have a basis in objective reality. If you tell your opponent that everyone has faced a raw materials cost increase over the past year and you're doing your best to keep costs down, it might help for you to show them a series of price sheets from some of your major competitors to indicate that, while everyone's prices have increased, yours have increased the least.

Take note: It can be dangerous to involve third parties in your negotiations, particularly third parties who have an interest in seeing your negotiation fail. For example, if you ask the person you are negotiating with to call your major competitor to find out their prices, your competitor may decide to steal your client away from you. If you ask someone to compare your prices with anyone else's prices, you'd better be aware that if she does find a better price, you may lose her as a client. If you tell a landlord that other apartments are renting for considerably less in the same neighborhood, the landlord may come back at you with a list of five apartments that rent for more. And then she might rent it to another person anyway, someone who causes less trouble and doesn't "call her a liar."

Sometimes offering Strategic Education can adversely affect the tone of a negotiation. People can misinterpret your offer of information as an attempt to hoodwink or insult them. They might think you are trying to show up their lack of knowledge about their own product or industry. How education is handled is just as important as what education consists of. Look at the two following attempts at Strategic Education and predict which one is going to be more successful.

Negotiation 1

"Lee—I've got some problems with your numbers here."

"What kind of problems?"

"Big problems. You're stealing from me with these prices."

"I've never stolen anything in my life."

"I called up Rocco's supply company—they say I should only pay twenty bucks for those gears. Your proposal asks for thirty-three!"

"But those numbers include a lot more!"

"Sure. But I don't need the copper handles. If you used steel, you could've saved me thirty-five more bucks. You never said anything, you swindler!"

"You never asked about steel!"

"You know what I mean. You're just in it for the money."

"That's unfair. I've done great work for you."

"And who knows how much money you've stolen from me in the past. Fifty dollars for tubing? I called a supply store and they quoted me $44, and I'm not even a professional!"

"But they don't install anything!"

"It takes one hour to install. You're ripping me off, right and left, and now you want to lump it all in the install section of the bill."

"I'm outta here. You're crazy!"

"You know I'm right. If you lower your bill, I'll consider taking you back."

Negotlation 2

"Lee—I'm having some trouble understanding some of your numbers here. If you can help me make some sense of them, I'd really appreciate it."

"Sure, Bill. What do you need to know?"

"Well, overall, the costs are running higher than I'd like."

"I'm giving you the best price I can. It's all the cost of the materials. That's what's driving your price up."

"Is there any way we can cut down on material costs?"

"Yeah, we can replace the copper handles. Those are always more expensive than steel."

"That'd be fine with me. What about the gears? How much do they run?"

"Oh, I get them for forty, forty-five dollars apiece. I'm not making much money on them."

"You know, I bet I can get them cheaper for you at this place I know. I'll check on the price and get back to you. If I can get them cheaper, we can both pay less for them."

"Sounds great to me."

"If I find I can get any of the other materials cheaply, I'll give you a call."

"Excellent."

The information exchanged was roughly the same, but each negotiation had a radically different outcome. When using Strategic Education, be aware of people's reactions. Give the other side all the opportunities you can to identify the problems themselves and come up with their own solutions. Introduce your own information only after they've shown a lack of understanding or don't have any solutions. Offer your information as if it weren't something they would be expected to know. In this way, they can save face and feel as if they were informed. This will set a productive precedent of solving problems by coming up with innovative solutions.

Negotiating Workshop #6

Strategic Education, No Extra Information, or Referral to Third Party?

For each of the following negotiation situations, decide whether you should educate, whether you should ask to be educated, or whether you should enlist a third party for educational purposes.

1. You are selling a car to a first-time buyer.
   - (A) Strategic Education
   - (B) Third Party
   - (C) No Extra Info

2. You are renegotiating a contract with a parts supplier of twenty years.
   - (A) Strategic Education
   - (B) Third Party
   - (C) No Extra Info

3. You are selling a new soft drink to kids.
   - (A) Strategic Education
   - (B) Third Party
   - (C) No Extra Info

4. You are offering a competitive bid on a construction job.
   - (A) Strategic Education
   - (B) Third Party
   - (C) No Extra Info

5. You are buying an apartment from a very large real estate firm.
   - (A) Strategic Education
   - (B) Third Party
   - (C) No Extra Info

CHAPTER 5

Creativity

If you think deals are just about price, you're in for a rude awakening. Of course price is a crucial part of any negotiation. But whenever you focus only on a single part of the negotiation, you're going to run into problems. A deal should be evaluated based on all of its terms—price, timing, payment, size, penalties, and everything else— or you're going to miss some potential benefits hidden within the deal.

A common but misguided mindset for negotiators is to keep their sights set on exact terms they want to emerge from the deal with. They repeat to themselves: "Twenty percent, ten thousand dollars, twenty percent, ten thousand dollars." By the time they walk into the negotiation, they've lost the ability to accept anything other than twenty percent and ten thousand dollars. It's alright to say that you're not going to accept less than twenty percent and ten thousand dollars. But you also need to keep your mind open to possible offers that would be even more valuable to you than twenty percent and ten thousand dollars.

This is why your negotiation plan is only a rough guide. If you are tied to exactly what you've written down on the page, you're closing off a host of possibilities you may not have thought of before. Let's say you're stuck on twenty percent, ten thousand dollars, and you're offered twice the amount of work for twenty percent and fifteen thousand dollars. You've hit your desired price, but at what value for the work? What if you're offered half the amount of work for thirty percent and five thousand dollars? It's less than you wanted, but do you really want to turn down an offer that may be more valuable than what you would have accepted on a different scale?

Once you've begun negotiating, it's very difficult to change your opinion about what some part of the deal is worth, so it is important to scrutinize each aspect of the deal before you get to the negotiating table. In the deal that follows, how responsive is Steve likely to be to Dave's changing opinion about the value of his stuff?

"O.K. Steve. This is it. I want $400 for the television and the VCR."

"Dave—I'm not going to pay more than $300."

"Then you aren't getting my T.V. and VCR."

"How about I give you $200 for the television?"

"How about you give me $300 for the television?"

"Then how about I give you $100 for the VCR?"

"How about you give me $200 for the VCR?"

"But that makes the two of them together $500!"

"You see! I'm giving you $100 off, because you're a friend."

"O.K. How about I give you $250 for the television."

"But then I'm stuck with the VCR. What good is a VCR if I have no television?"

"You can use it as a doorstop."

"Yeah, a $300 doorstop."

"I thought you said it was $200."

"That's before I remembered you could use it as a doorstop, too."

Steve is probably through dealing with Dave at this point. The more creative you can be before the negotiating process begins, the more flexible you can be once it starts. Keep yourself open to all alternatives the other side proposes, and explore your own creative side too. The more open-minded you can be in your approaches to negotiation, the more likely the two parties will come to a mutually acceptable solution.

CREATIVITY EXERCISE #1

By increasing your general intellectual creativity, you will approach any negotiating situation better equipped. Here's a quick workout to gauge the flexibility of your thinking. Imagine the following scenario. You are in a room with floors and walls made of wood. There is no furniture in the room, except for a large fishtank right in the middle. At the bottom of that fishtank is a diamond worth one million dollars. There are sleeping guards in every corner. If there is any loud noise, they will wake up and arrest you. All you have to do is retrieve the diamond from the bottom of the fishtank. Oh, and the fishtank is full of flesh-eating piranha fish. You have with you the following items:

1. a wad of cotton
2. a hammer
3. a straw
4. a cup
5. a steel canister
6. a side of beef
7. a stack of paper plates
8. a towel
9. a baseball bat

Write down all the ways that you can think of to retrieve the diamond without waking the guards or getting your arm chewed off.

Creativity means opening yourself up to new solutions. When you negotiate, you should be creative in three ways: you should be flexible, be a careful listener, and be able to assign value.

Flexibility

We've said it before, but it's worth saying again: Going into any negotiation with a rigid sense of what you want makes negotiating more difficult and more likely to fail than if you are flexible. Stay open to finding new solutions to existing problems, even when those solutions are not on your negotiation plan. When you remain flexible, you'll never let a deal fail unless it simply can't be done at all.

A flexible stance does not mean accepting a deal below your trip wires or letting yourself be railroaded into a solution that creates more problems for you than benefits. On the contrary, flexibility opens up the negotiation to a better solution for all parties. For example, in 1993, basketball player Nick Van Exel was drafted out of the University of Cincinnati by the Los Angeles Lakers. Though an accomplished college player, Van Exel is only six feet tall and had demonstrated questionable shot selection, making his value uncertain. The Lakers offered him the standard contract for a player drafted in his position, although at a slightly lower price than the market might have determined. Van Exel, however, had a different belief

---

11

Or Else

Identification
When the other side says "or else," you're under the pressure of a threat. You know it. They know it. But what are you going to do about it?

Note
Threats only work when the person making them:
1. Doesn't care about the relationship.
2. Can back them up.
3. Is prepared to back them up.

Solution
It is often more effective to address the other side's tone than to focus on the substance of what they say. A simple "we can work this out without threats," usually makes the other side state exactly what they want. If they can and will back up their threats, you might have to decide that the deal does not satisfy your needs and consider the negotiation closed at that point.

in the worth of his skills. Contract talks stalled on a long-term contract until his agent decided to be creative. The agent stopped arguing price and length of contract and offered the Lakers a one-year contract at the league minimum—way below even the Lakers's original offer—to give Van Exel a chance to prove his skills. The Lakers found this interesting. If he proved himself during the season, they would pay fair market value for his services from that point on; if he turned out to be less talented than they believed, they would save themselves a lot of money. There was an additional benefit to the Lakers in signing the kind of contract Van Exel signed. Each NBA team is limited in the amount of money they can offer in any given year by a "salary cap" of roughly twelve million dollars. By signing Van Exel at the league minimum—$109,000—they kept more money available to sign other free agents. And if a team re-signs a player who played for them the year before, that money doesn't count toward the salary cap. Van Exel ended up having an excellent year and signed a five-year deal with the Lakers for over ten million dollars.

In this case, Van Exel took a big risk, betting on his skills and his continuing health, and it paid off. His range of alternatives was expanded by his willingness to take that risk. Not all such gambles are successful, however. A recent case of risk-taking behavior that did not pay off is Danny Manning, another basketball player, who was offered over three million dollars a year to remain with the Atlanta Hawks. He decided he wanted a championship ring more than guaranteed money, so he elected to leave the Hawks and sign with a team that had a strong chance to contend for an NBA title. He signed a one-year deal with the Phoenix Suns for below his market value, since they were close to the salary cap for that year. Manning expected that after the year was up, he would sign a long-term, multi-million dollar deal with the Suns. During the season, he tore the anterior cruciate ligament in his knee. Unfortunately for Manning, he will never play as well or command that kind of money again, and it is unlikely that the Phoenix Suns will re-sign him for next season.

Many large companies have "Creative Blockbusting Sessions" where they invite workers from all levels to come up with solutions to company problems. "There are no bad solutions," one executive says, "only ones we choose not to implement." Most of the suggestions range from the impossible to the bizarre, but even the most outlandish suggestion often contains the kernel of an idea that proves valuable. One cost-cutting creative blockbusting session for a pharmaceutical company came up with the following solutions:

1. *Free employee samples to improve worker productivity*
2. *No more toilet paper*
3. *Sell chairs & tables*
4. *Company rodeo to raise money*
5. *Raise insurance level then burn factory down*

Ideas number 1 and 4 ended up leading to an employee discount for products and group events, both of which raised worker morale and productivity.

The point is that flexibility and innovative thinking go hand-in-hand. Solutions are created all the time in ways that not only meet the needs of each party, but also expand the gains that each party can make. Ask yourself these questions:

1. **Am I resistant to an offer merely because I didn't think of it?**

   It's not unusual to resent someone who thinks of something you didn't. Aim to make an accurate, informed, objective judgment about the fairness of an offer without regard to who came up with it first. You might try imagining that you yourself were planning to propose this solution to the negotiation in order to put yourself in the frame of mind to evaluate the offer on its merits alone. What would the benefits be to your side? How would it address your needs? How would it address their needs?

2. **Is the other side thinking creatively?**

   If the other side is locked into a "one issue/one solution" negotiating position, they are going to be limited in their ability to suggest alternative solutions. Obviously, you can't force another side to think creatively—though you'll often wish you could. What you can do, however, is educate them about your creative suggestions. Perhaps something you'll say or

12

The Non-Negotiators

Identification
The other party refuses to negotiate and discuss terms with you. They submit a proposal with a price and terms and then ask you to accept or reject it on the whole.

Note
A refusal to negotiate is usually a refusal to negotiate price. This is an opportunity for you. Since they are rigid on price, you can ask for concessions on other terms. Asking for clarification as to why they won't negotiate will usually let you know where there is some room for discussion. If they continue to not negotiate, you may consider choosing another company and telling the original one that had they been more willing to negotiate, they may have gotten your business.

Solution
Approach them in a positive and inquisitive way. Tell them you'd love to make a deal, but you have some questions. Don't try to negotiate right away. They will take the time to educate you. When they commit some time and energy to your education, they suddenly have more at stake in the discussions. Then, when you have more information and some creative alternatives to approach them with, they'll be more willing to bargain. Sometimes how you do something is just as important as what you do.

offer will start them thinking about the deal in completely new terms. Tell them about different ways in which your needs could be satisfied. In other words, give them some raw material that they can mull over later. One important element in any negotiation is time—and we'll discuss how to use time to your advantage in chapter 6. But if the other side isn't thinking creatively, a good idea is to throw some suggestions to the other side and then recess. Give them some time to let your ideas sink in. They may even be inspired by your ingenuity to come up with their own creative proposals.

3. **Am I being flexible or am I being a pushover?**
   The downside of flexibility is that in your desire to consider every possible option, you may send inappropriate signals to the other side. In chapter 5, we'll talk about what benchmarks you should use to determine value. But be aware that flexibility means openness—not acquiescence. When an offer is made that is completely unacceptable to you, make certain that when you reject it, you make your reasons clear.

> *In their zeal to avoid a salary cap, NHLPA representatives compromised on every issue important to the other side. The rules on arbitration, free-agency, and rookie salaries were all changed to meet the owners' demands. In many ways, the salary cap that the NHL didn't get would have caused less pain to the players than the conglomeration of new rules did. By focusing on a single issue rather than the overall picture, the Players' Association lost out.*

Listening

Larry is wandering through an electronics store, and he notices a stereo on sale—a tuner, a tape player, and a set of speakers—for $300. Chuck, the salesperson, sees him approaching and offers his hand.

"So this stereo set is on sale for $300?"

"Yup. Do you want one of them, or two?"

"I'm just looking. Is there anything I should know about this set?"

"It's a great deal. I'd get better speakers though."

"Can I substitute better speakers?"

"Nope."

"Does a CD player come with this stereo set?"

"Nope."

"Is there any way to get this price down?"

"Not really."

"No way at all."

"Nope."

"Thanks for your time."

Flexibility is intimately tied to being a careful listener. Listen raptly to the offers someone proposes and the terms he gives you. For example, if a salesperson keeps talking about "the best deal you'll ever get, the most for your money, the finest craftsmanship, the most elegant materials," and doesn't get to the price for a long, long time, be patient. Let him give you a hundred reasons for his price. That never precludes you from taking issue with it. Additionally, you now have a hundred reasons to attack the price and ask for a lower one. By listening carefully, you can determine what the other side's needs are, and you are in a better position to offer a creative alternative. Look at how the above scenario changes when both sides listen better and think more flexibly:

"My name's Chuck. Can I help you with anything?"

"My name's Larry. Just looking at this stereo."

"It's a great stereo. If you want more depth to the sound, though, I'd get better speakers."

"And how much would those cost?"

"About $200 more."

"Two hundred dollars more? That almost doubles the price!"

"You get what you pay for. Now look, my boss doesn't want you to know this, but those speakers they include with the package . . . ? They're lousy. You can barely hear any drums in the background."

"Then why do they include them?"

"How are you gonna sell a stereo without speakers?"

"You've got a point. But I can't pay $500 for this system. It doesn't even have a CD player. Can you do something about the price?"

"I wish I could. You see, on all these sale items, us salespeople have very little room to drop the price. If I sell you one of these things, I make twenty, maybe thirty dollars. The store only makes about forty. But the quality sucks."

"What if I buy a different stereo? Could you give me a break on the price? That way you get better commission and I get a better deal."

"I could do that if you get that CD player you talked about as well. I can get you better speakers and—heck, better everything— for about the same amount of money."

"And you know, I've got a couple of friends who are looking for good equipment themselves. If you can give me a good deal here, I'll send them over."

"I am sure we can find an excellent deal for you."

By starting with the basic assumption that the price was negotiable, the buyer sent a clear signal to the salesperson—no way this deal gets done on these terms at this price. The salesperson uses Strategic Education to inform the buyer about the product and the pricing. He also provides a piece of information—he makes less commission on sale items—that allows the buyer to offer a creative solution to their mutual needs. Note that this important piece of information was obtained because Larry was listening carefully and managed to discern and then work with Chuck's desire for a higher commission.

13 *Upping the Ante*

Identification
You ask for a small concession. The other side agrees—if you'll make a major concession on something else. You refuse. You ask for another small concession. They ask for another major one in return. Pretty soon, you're tired of asking for anything. They've made it impossible for you to get any more concessions.

Note
Upping the ante can lead to renegotiation of an entire contract, so be careful. Policies of escalation can create ill will and lead you places you don't want to go. However, when someone keeps asking for tips, a few "ante-uppers" should stop that behavior.

Solution
As with all irrational negotiating tactics, bringing the policy to light may have a positive effect. Another way to defuse an "upping the ante" situation is to do the same yourself. Respond to their disproportionate requests with your own, absurdly high requests. After a time, you'll both be able to proceed in a reasonable, productive fashion.

Negotiating Workshop #7

Careful Listening

Read the following sentences and decide how important each might be to a negotiation, on a scale of 1 to 10. Remember: Careful listening can open the door to creative solutions.

1. "You know, I'm on the spot here. My manager is waiting to see if we make a deal."
2. "I'm not allowed to go any lower on price."
3. "At these volumes, I'm not making any money."
4. "You know, I ski too, and those skis you're looking at—they're for beginners. They're not for an expert like you."
5. "I'll take your offer to my boss, but I don't think he'll like it."
6. "Make me a better offer."
7. "You know, prices are going up all the time. When's the last time you heard of prices going down?"
8. "I only have three left in that color. They're going fast..."
9. "That product comes all the way from Russia. Do you know how much it takes to ship this from Russia?"
10. "I'm indifferent between the up-front money and the percentage. Either one is good for me."

Assigning Value

Assigning value is how you decide what you want, not just when you negotiate, but in all aspects of your life. Something that's valuable to you is something you want. Something that's less valuable is something you don't want as much. Before you enter any negotiation, you've got to look at every part of a deal and ask yourself, "What's it worth to me?" Your answers don't have to be the most specific ones in the world, like "$372.12" or "On a scale of 1 to 10, I'd rank this a 6.53." But the values you assign should be distinguishable. Just being able to determine if something is "very" valuable or "not very" valuable can guide you through dangerous waters in any deal.

Always remember that each person is going to answer the question "What's it worth to me?" according to his own needs. Don't assume that the other person has the exact same opinion you do on the value of every part of a deal, or you're going to find yourself giving away things that could have been worth more to you than to him. The other person is the only one who knows what he values most. Your job is to find out as much about what he values as you can.

You'll find that pinpointing differences in assigning value is the basis of all "win/win" negotiations. By discovering differences in your valuations, you can actually find areas that make both parties content. If you think something is not very valuable, but the other side thinks it is very valuable, you can probably get something important to you in return for it.

Taking an inflexible position in a public forum can lock you into a stance antithetical to a creative compromise. As the NFL Players Union contract expired, Gene Upshaw, president of the union, and the league owners engaged in a mud-slinging contest in the national press that made each side less willing to modify its position. The result? The players struck, while the owners locked out the players and brought in scab replacements. These replacement players were such poor substitutes that coaches were forced to use "trick" plays that are rarely seen in the NFL, such as the "Statue of Liberty" play.

Let's look at an example. You are a software programmer who has designed the perfect system for Company X. The only thing is, they want you to train their employees to use the system. For you, training their employees is a snap. It'll take you a couple of days at most, and you already know everything about the system. You assign very little value to training Company X's employees. Company X, however, knows that without training, this great system they have is useless. They are willing to pay a bunch of money to have their people trained by the one person who knows the system inside and out. They assign a very high value to your training of their employees. By trading your item of low value to you for one of high value to them, you can get something you value more, cash, and they can get the expert training they desire. In this case, both parties come out ahead.

Now, no one is going to go into a negotiation and state, "This is what I want most, this second, and this last." Doing that will give away critical information that may allow the other side to extract huge concessions from you for the one thing you want most. You've got to keep your valuations as hidden as possible while figuring out what the other side's are. But if you can find a way to get at value for both parties, you've got a winning solution.

Value and creativity go hand-in-hand. The negotiator who can be most creative about finding value is, in the long run, going to be the most successful. Some place you might look for hidden value in a negotiation are:

1. Size—if the volume or scale changes, how will that affect the other parts of the deal?
2. Timing—when is the deal going to get done?
3. Payment—how much, when, what form? Cash or credit?
4. Penalties—who is responsible if something goes wrong?
5. Support—if we have question, who can we call? How often?
6. Features—is there something unusual involved?
7. Location—if location is an issue, how can you turn it into value?

Negotiating Workshop #8

Increasing Options

In the following deadlocked deal, there are a number of unusual options available to each side. You don't have to identify the offer that each side would make, but try to identify the areas that each side should be looking to for creative possibilities.

An executive at Meghan Industries wants to lease a car from a local car company. The car is large, has four doors, and is painted a classic black. The owner of the car company normally rents this car for $35 per day. The executive needs it for three days this week and three days the next week. He rents cars regularly and has cash or credit available. He wants to direct his business locally, but if he can't find a car at the right price, he'll go with a national firm. The owner of the car company knows that the executive wants to rent a car but has no other information. The executive has offered $20 per day for the same car. The negotiations are currently stalled.

CHAPTER 6

Ready, Willing, and Wait a Minute

This chapter looks at all the things you must think about before you step into the bargaining room. We'll discuss hardball, timing, and formulating your first offer. If you go into the negotiation without thinking about these three things, you're running an unnecessary risk.

> Hardball – *[pr. 'Hahrd-bawl']* 1) a game played by professionals involving dense circular projectiles propelled at speeds in excess of 90 miles per hour in which, at any given time, a team of people wearing spikes opposes another team of people wearing spikes, and one team is allowed to wield a cylinder of lumber and swing it as hard as they can. 2) a negotiating strategy that involves a similar amount of risk.

To unilaterally demand an agreement, with little room for concessions, is to play hardball. Often, playing hardball means setting strict time limits. Such phrases as "take it or leave it," and "it's this or nothing," make clear one side's willingness to walk away from the negotiations. Playing hardball can be dangerous, exciting, and profitable, but it can also result in complete failure. More than with any other technique, the decision to play hardball or not is all-important. Play hardball in an ill-advised situation and you lose everything—the deal at hand as well as future deals and possibly the good will of the other side. Hardball is called for only when it has a good chance of getting you all the gains you want. Ask yourself these questions:

1. If the negotiation fails, do you have other alternatives or are you equally satisfied with no deal? Does a deal make no sense to you except within a certain set of parameters? If so, you're in a good position to play hardball. For example, you own a house and someone drives through your neighborhood looking for a place to live. He knocks on your door and offers you a certain amount for your house. Now, you were not looking to sell your house. You are perfectly content to live in the house forever. But someone comes along and offers you money you didn't expect. For a high enough sum, you'd consider moving. Why not play hardball under these circumstances? If you don't get the exact terms you want, you can walk away with no problem.

2. Is the other side susceptible to hardball? You have to gauge how the other side will respond to hardball tactics. Are they under some kind of deadline pressure? What are their alternatives to your involvement? If you are one of ten people bidding on a piece of antique furniture, playing hardball won't work at all. If you are the only person bidding and they really want to get rid of the piece, it might. Hardball tactics only work when the other side has few alternatives and is under considerable pressure.

3. How will this affect future relationships with the other party? You may not want to play hardball if you have to maintain a good relationship with the other side. If you play hardball, expect to use up any good will you've accrued to that point. Hardball negotiations can go sour very quickly and leave a nasty aftertaste.

Keep hardball negotiating in your arsenal of techniques, and if the situation calls for it, don't be afraid to use it. Under the right circumstances, you can get a deal that you would otherwise never get—just be sure you know how to recognize the right circumstances.

"Hey Mike—I'm calling you to see if you've made a decision on my offer."

"I'm thinking about it, Carlos. It's not everything I'd like."

"Well then, make me a counteroffer."

"I made you my first offer. Then you came back at me with this. Why did you think my position would change?"

"It's just that it's coming up on the end of the year, and I'd like to be able to tell my kids we've bought a great ski cabin in Vermont."

"I'd love to be able to help you, Carlos, but I've really got to think about it."

"I'll tell you what—I'll give you three thousand more. But that's all I can pay."

"That's great. I'll think about it."

"You'll think about it? I'm offering you more money."

"And I'm going to think about it."

"What do you want? What more could you want?"

Mike and Carlos are running into a common problem that takes hold of deals and pressures one side or another into making a decision. Each side places a different value on the timing of the deal. Timing is one of the most important features of any negotiation and it pays to figure out how to use it to your advantage. Many negotiators make the mistake of assuming that the pace and the timing of their deal has no effect on the outcome. Large-scale and small-scale negotiations alike rely heavily on timing, and the success or failure of many negotiations can be directly related to how smart one side is in using timing to their advantage.

History is rife with examples of different groups using timing to their advantage in negotiations. Perhaps the most striking examples of the potency of timing as a bargaining tool occur during union negotiations. When a union decides to negotiate a new contract with a company, it generally holds off beginning discussions until the old contract is about to expire. Union negotiators know that if they wait until the end of the old contract to begin negotiating, the company will be forced to lend an air of seriousness and urgency to the proceedings. If the company stalls, they can expect to face a number of days where no workers show up to the factory. Thus every day the company doesn't make any progress in the negotiations is another day that the company has to shut down its factory and lose a lot of money.

On the other hand, once the factory has shut down for a few days, the company starts to think about the union's general strike fund. They may not return to the negotiating table for a number of weeks, until they feel the union has begun to run out of money. At this point, they can expect members who need money desperately to urge their union to reach a settlement on any terms. Then they might return to the negotiating table. Things can drag out to the point where both sides have lost much more than they were prepared to lose.

> *Han Solo played hardball and won. Harrison Ford was doing so well in his Hollywood carpentry business that when he was offered the role of Han Solo in the famous Star Wars series of movies, he almost turned it down. He was prepared to not take the role if the terms were not appealing to him. He always had his carpentry business to fall back on. Eventually, they offered him the terms he wanted. As risky as Ford's move was, it paid off, and now we can't think of Han Solo being played by anyone else.*

You can use timing to help you during your own negotiations. All it takes is some preparation, some information, and some courage. Why courage? Because if you are going to use timing to your best advantage, you have to be prepared to play a little hardball and ask for better terms with less flexibility. If the negotiations go on longer than you anticipate, timing may swing to your disadvantage. In other words, these techniques aren't for the faint of heart. In the company vs. union example above, a stalled negotiation can mean the company may have to shut down. On the other hand, the company may choose to replace the striking workers with "scabs," either for the duration of the negotiation or permanently. This move may force workers, who fear the "substitute" workers will take over their jobs, either to end the strike, or, sometimes, resort to violence. Remember that hardball negotiations can escalate quickly into high-stake negotiations.

Pressuring the other side by using timing can be tremendously effective. In the short term, the other side has great incentive to negotiate and to make concessions. In the long term, however, don't be surprised if they use timing pressure on you in the next bargaining session.

Understanding the other side's concept of the length of the negotiation is another clue that can help you understand their negotiating styles. If someone is coming to town to negotiate a deal with you, call her hotel. How long is she registered for? Does the other side expect a two-day negotiation? A two-week negotiation? Understanding her expectations will help you judge her attitude toward the deal.

Before negotiating, you should always find out as much as possible about the time pressures that exist on the other side. For example, you may be negotiating a lease with a landlord who has a policy that all leases will begin on the first of the month. If the negotiations extend into the next month, the landlord may be losing a month's rent. So the landlord may push to finish the negotiations before the

14 Exhaustion

Identification
The negotiation goes on all day long. At the end of the day, when you are close to an agreement, the other side presents you with an offer that you probably could agree to, although it doesn't completely fulfill your needs. Tired and fed up, you accept the agreement rather than spend another day negotiating.

Note
This policy is used all the time by people, companies and even countries negotiating long-term agreements. Professional negotiators never fail to recognize that the other parties are people and subject to exhaustion, anger, and impatience to make a deal. They use this knowledge to their advantage.

Solution
Never be afraid to ask for breaks or to reconvene the negotiations at another time. Point out your fatigue and let them know that you'd be more than willing to go over their proposal in the morning. No one can hold you in that negotiating room for one minute more than you are willing to stay. Rush decisions can be fatal. It's worthwhile to review any document with a clean hand before you agree to the terms contained in it.

first. By understanding the pressure that is on him to sign the lease by the end of the month, you know that small concessions you ask for, which he might ordinarily balk at, might not be contested. Or a supplier may be evaluated monthly by his boss. If you've spent most of the month negotiating with him and you haven't reached an agreement, he may be under even more pressure to reach an agreement by the end of the month. But beware! If you don't reach an agreement and he has to explain to his boss that he's spending two months on this negotiation, he may be under pressure to bring in one heck of a contract. Timing is useful, but it can work against you just as easily as it can work for you.

Whenever you negotiate, you have to look at the whole deal, and to do that, you need time. Don't corner yourself into a quick negotiation. Quick negotiations don't give you enough of an opportunity to analyze and examine the offers presented to you, nor do they give you the chance to propose creative alternatives. Quick negotiations force hasty decisions without much thought given to satisfying or taking care of each party's needs.

What kinds of negotiations tend to be quick negotiations? Deals that take place over the telephone, renegotiations of existing contracts, negotiations between friends, and "special offers." Whenever possible, avoid making deals over the telephone. Negotiating over the phone lends itself to slapdash decisions. It is much easier to communicate with someone when you're together in a room. For one thing, over the telephone, there's a limited amount of body-language information you can give or receive. Existing contracts or annual supplier contracts also tend to be done too fast since they are usually just re-approvals of existing terms. But it's worth your time to examine these contracts one by one and term by term. Your needs change over time, and your contracts should reflect your current needs. Deals between friends are delicate ones that also tend to be rushed. You don't want to create any ill will through protracted negotiations, but you want a deal that works to your advantage. Keep in mind that the best way to preserve a good, long-term relationship is to negotiate a meticulous deal that spells out everything in detail and satisfies both parties' needs.

Look out for the "special offer" deals. Special offer bargains are intended to do a couple of things. One, they bring you into a store or introduce you to a company's services. Usually, the firm has priced the good or service close to cost, just to drag you in. This is commonly known in retail as a "loss leader." The goal is to introduce you to the company, not make any money. If you don't have any obligation to negotiate anything else, go ahead. In this case, it is alright to conclude a deal quickly. If there are other, longer term ramifications, take whatever time you need to examine the deal. If the offer expires in the meanwhile, relax. For every good deal you shouldn't let pass by you, there are three that you definitely should let get away. It makes sense to take time to really investigate your options.

"Dana—I've got approval to offer you $5000 for the paperback rights to your book, if you sign the contract today. I was told if you don't accept right away, I'll have to take the offer off the table."

"Jill—I appreciate the higher offer, and I am optimistic that we can reach a deal, but I've got to think about this. Let me call you back."

"It's either now or never."

"So the rights are worth $5000 this second, but a few minutes later, they'll be worth less? That doesn't make sense. Give me a few minutes, let me figure out what your offer gives me, and I'll get back to you later today."

"What'll I tell my boss?"

"Tell him I was in a meeting and you won't be able to get me until the afternoon. I should have an answer by then."

"O.K. But don't call my boss. Call me with an answer by five."

"I can do that. Thanks for the time."

A deal may seem a good one immediately, but when you take a little time to think about it, sometimes it turns out to be a bad deal. Perhaps, in the above deal, Dana wanted five thousand dollars for her book and another two thousand for the movie rights. Without the paperback rights, she is in a less advantageous position when it's time to sell the movie rights. This new "take it or leave it" offer may actually be worse than a more comprehensive offer for both rights. By taking some time to review the offer, Dana can assign it its proper value.

Short negotiations encourage bad behavior: quick decisions, deadlines, ultimatums, stifled creativity. Short negotiations, then, usually lead to a one-sided outcome—one side emerges much better off than the other. Do you want to ask the other person to negotiate quickly? If you are more prepared, able to evaluate the deal quicker, and can dictate the terms that the other side is considering, then why not? Quick negotiations offer you an opportunity to conclude an agreement to one party's advantage. If that party is you, then by all means, negotiate quickly. Remember, though, if you expect a long-term relationship with the person involved, it works to both your advantages to come out with a winning solution for all parties.

15 Rotating Negotiators

Identification
You negotiate a deal with someone, and get fairly good terms. Then another person replaces the first negotiator, saying that it has all been a mistake. That person shouldn't have been assigned to your contract. This time, you get acceptable terms. Then a new person shows up and says he apologizes, but you should have been negotiating with him in the first place. At this point, you are ready to give in on any terms to get a deal signed by someone with authority.

Note
Rotating negotiators can work to break another party's will and to get you information about the other side's position. Negotiating the same contract twice or three times is exhausting. But the cost is a large loss in credibility. If you are involved in a continuing relationship with the other party, you may not want to use this tactic.

Solution
As you begin any negotiation, ask the following questions of the other side:

1. Are you the appointed negotiator for your company?
2. Do you have the authority to agree to terms and to sign the contract for your company?

If the answer to either of these questions is no, you should ask to speak with someone who does have the authority to sign contracts. Right up front explain that you don't want to go through this negotiation twice. Be honest about your expectations—not for the outcome, but for the negotiation itself.

NEGOTIATING WORKSHOP #9

Taking Time

In each of the following negotiations, does the timing work to your benefit or your detriment?

1. The contract you are working under expires at midnight.
2. You have just signed a lease with a landlord and you are negotiating for an extra year.
3. You are submitting a competitive bid to a potential client.
4. You are negotiating a December ski vacation with a travel agency in August.
5. You are asking for a raise as your company's stock hits an all-time low.
6. You are asking for a raise as your company's stock hits an all-time high.
7. You are moving in a week and you are selling your furniture.
8. You are selling your apartment but have not found a new place to live.
9. You are purchasing a house that was just featured in a national magazine as "one of the ten most beautiful mansions in the U.S."
10. You are buying a new tank of oxygen for your iron lung as the old one dwindles to nothing.

There's another benefit from an extended negotiation. Remember how people feel about the supermarket. When they complain about the prices, they aren't merely complaining about the money involved. They're complaining about their lack of say in the prices. The advantage of negotiating is that each party spends time, energy, and effort to reach a final goal. The more each party contributes to a deal, the more they each have a stake in continuing the communication and remaining creative and flexible.

It's always a good idea to decide your timing based on the other side's needs, not your own. Suppliers and purchasers, for example, do this all the time. Suppliers of a product tend to want to negotiate new contracts just as you begin to run out of supplies. They reason, understandably, that you won't come back to your boss saying, "Sorry, boss, we don't have any paper clips this week because I'm trying to get him down a tenth of a cent per item." Timing will work against you if you depend on a continuous supply of something. If the deal falls through and there's no product, who do you think your boss will blame? You or your vendor?

Purchasers, however, try to negotiate terms on a long-term basis long before their supplies dwindle in the event the negotiation is protracted. They try to take some time between negotiations to test the market and meet with other suppliers to discuss terms, price, and quantities. Even if you have a good relationship with a supplier, you owe it to yourself to check the market every now and then. Prices may get better with technological improvement and cost reductions. Vendors are more willing to negotiate terms if they know that you have been testing the waters and are considering leaving them.

Choose your timing well. By giving the other side a sense of the urgency of getting to the negotiating table, you can find terms that will help you get the most from any bargaining session.

The final thing you should do before beginning a negotiation is examine your requests. Have a first offer prepared before you step into the negotiating room. Ask yourself, am I dealing with the right amount of money? It can be difficult to be aggressive in making your first offer for anything. Making an absurdly low offer or asking a ridiculously high price establishes you as an irrational negotiator and angers the other side.

It's up to you to decide on the amount of your own initial offers, and so long as you don't stray into the ridiculous, there is nothing wrong with an aggressive initial valuation. You're better off if you overvalue your own product rather than undervalue it, just as it's better to undervalue someone else's product than overvalue it.

You need to make your best guess, because no matter how much you prepare for a negotiation, you cannot predict the other side's valuation. There's psychology involved here as well. Simply put, the more you believe you deserve to get, the more likely you are to come out with a satisfying deal. Try it out. When you are absolutely convinced that you should get better terms, and you're consistent and continuous in your efforts to get those better terms, you are much more likely to bring the other side around to your point of view.

Bill Cosby sets his expectations high. To return for a seventh season as the charming father of the Huxtable family, he requested a $100 million bonus. He also asked that NBC take on the cost of producing the show, which had previously cost Carsey-Werner, Cosby's production company, about a million dollars per show. Bill Cosby's demands sound outrageous, until you understand that the show takes in around four million per episode in advertising revenue. Although exact terms weren't disclosed, Cosby was very happy with the $52-million deal his production company eventually struck with NBC.

Defense attorneys are experts at using aggressiveness to their advantage. During a criminal trial, nearly every time the prosecution makes an error in fact, the defense attorneys put on record that their client has been "irreparably harmed" and demand a mistrial. They don't necessarily expect to get a mistrial—although they would love that. In part, the defense attorneys are looking to preserve the right to appeal by putting it on record, but by asking for the most stringent reprimand available, they sway the judge toward a harsh penalty while still being able to point to the fact that the judge didn't, in fact, grant the mistrial. By asking for an aggressive sanction, defense attorneys reduce the prosecution's expectation that they will get away with errors.

Be aggressive in your first offers. Every new teacher is given some good advice: begin strict—you can always loosen up later, but it's difficult to get control of a class back once you've lost it. The same holds true for negotiations. If you go in there tough, considering your options, and with full knowledge of your opponent's position, you're going to come out a winner.

CHAPTER 7

The Main Event

"It's showtime!"
—Roy Scheider playing
Bob Fosse in *All That Jazz*

When you walk into the negotiating room or meet the person you are going to be negotiating with, keep in mind the following facts: You have done your preparation, you can communicate well, you've adopted a flexible mindset, you know how to use Strategic Education, and, if possible, you've structured the timing to your advantage. You know what your trip wires are, and you've got a good idea about what the other side is going to ask for. Get excited—you're ready to negotiate. You know exactly what you're going to do.

The problem, however, is what the other side is going to do. Negotiating well is a skill, and other parties may have achieved a good amount of success in the past by using tactics you've never seen before. You can expect them to try to use those tactics on you. But never fear. Even when faced with an unexpected move, you can still figure out a way to turn a tactic on its head.

You don't have to negotiate for twenty years to recognize the tactics that most people use. As you've no doubt noticed, the fifteen most common negotiating tactics are scattered throughout *Don't Be A Chump* in our negotiation tactic boxes so you can get used to them as you are learning the most important negotiating skills. In any real deal it's important that you know all of these tactics before you walk into the negotiation. So if you've skipped some, don't just go flipping back through the book. Below you'll find a list, with page references, of the main techniques you are likely to encounter.

If you aren't familiar with any of them, take the time now to go back to the negotiation tactic boxes and review those techniques. The more you know about these techniques and the more adept you are at recognizing them, the more easily you can turn them against the person trying to get you.

If you don't recognize the tactic, you're not going to know how to disarm it. One way to practice recognizing negotiation tactics is to have a friend try them out on you. You should first identify, then disarm the tactic. The faster you can identify a tactic against you, the more you can turn it to your advantage. Conversely, the longer you let a tactic go on without mentioning it, the more difficult it will be to stop it.

NEGOTIATING WORKSHOP #10

Identify the Tactic

Read the following excerpts from negotiations and identify what tactic one party is trying to use on the other party.

1.   *"You want an extra ten days to pay on the contract? I can give you the extra days if we double the price."*

2.   *"So I think we've come to common agreement on most of the major points. Why don't I have my office draw up a contract right now so we can get this deal done?"*

3.   *"You know, I'd love to make that change, but I'm going to have to run this by my boss, and you know he's really tough. I don't think he'll go for it."*

4.   *"Sorry about all the sunlight, but the window blinds broke yesterday and I haven't had a chance to get them fixed. Let's discuss the terms."*

5.   *"Our figures, based on our own careful research, indicate that by the year 1999, seventy-three percent of the American people will be vegetarian, so we see our market for soy burgers increasing by at least 900 percent. Look at the way this graph slopes upward. It's inevitable."*

6.   *"I know it's been a long day, but let's go over this one more time. If we can make one more push on some minor issues, I am highly confident that we can finish up the deal tonight."*

7.   *"I know that we're going to have to talk about the rent you want for this apartment and the term of the lease, but I think we have to talk about the no-pet clause. I'm a real believer in pets— I've had one all my life—but for this apartment I'm willing to give up my pet. I'm willing to install bars on the window to make this building more safe and secure. I also have some plumbing and repair skills, and I can fix up the apartment to make it in excellent condition. Now, let's talk about rent."*

8.   *"I'm sorry for all the confusion. Larry, the last person you were talking to doesn't have the authority to negotiate this contract. I'm the person you should have been negotiating with all along."*

9.   *"This is it. Either take it, or else I'll have to leave you as my supplier."*

10.   *"I'll tell you what. We need to show some cash up front, so if you sign this deal, I'll cut you ten—no fifteen—percent off the next deal when we negotiate it next year. If we don't, I'm not sure we're going to be around to negotiate anything next year."*

11.   *"You have our offer. If you have problems with it, I suggest you go somewhere else."*

12.   *"Take it easy, Charlie. I'm sure we don't want to blame David here if his offer wasn't what we wanted. He was just doing the best he could. Can I get you some coffee, David? I sympathize with your position—you're just trying to do your job. What I think Charlie means, his screaming aside, is that to do business, we're going to need a better offer, and I know that with all your creative knowledge, you'll be able to do better with the next one."*

13.   *"Sure we can accept your timing recommendations. I'll pass them on to the senior committee and they'll make a recommendation. Those will be passed along to the vice-president in charge of the division, who will form his own committee and then pass along a recommendation to the president. I don't see any problems, though."*

14.   *"If you don't accept our offer, I'll ruin your name in this business. You'll be looking for work in another country."*

15.   *"You know, I can sign this deal now if you can give me a custom color on this couch. I couldn't pay any more, but I'm ready to sign if you can give me a bright red rather than the white one here."*

During the negotiation, it may seem awkward to bring to light some of the other side's tactics. After all, you want to maintain a good relationship with them, and isn't accusing them of trying to use a tactic on you the same as accusing them of trying to cheat you? Relax. Just because someone tries to use experience to his advantage doesn't mean he is trying to cheat you, or that he is not worth negotiating with. It's up to you to respond. One excellent way to call attention to any unpleasant situation or touchy subject is to phrase it in the form of a question. A question is the least confrontational way of getting the other side to reexamine its position.

Negotiating Workshop #11

Using the Question

For each of the fifteen most common techniques, write a question that would defuse it or at least let the other side know that you're aware of it without giving offense.

While discussing the deal, be aware of how focused the other side is on the problem. If the other side has come to the negotiation with an adversarial outlook, you're going to have trouble getting them to think creatively. Small things you do during the negotiation can change their mindset while not altering a thing about each side's position. For example, sitting on one side of a table while the other party is sitting directly across from you makes the situation more confrontational. By sitting on the same side of a table, the two of you can be focused on the problems of the deal, not the conflicts between the negotiators. What if you are continuously interrupted by phone calls? Do you think this sends a message to the other side that you are serious and committed to the negotiation? Clear a time and a place for the negotiation, one that sends the appropriate message of seriousness and respect.

If you have bad news or are bargaining from a limited position, you should inform the other side as soon as you begin to discuss terms. There is nothing more frustrating than spending time trying to establish your position only to later find out that they never had the ability to modify their position at all. If you know that you cannot accept a certain term, you should tell the other side first, so that it never enters the discussion and so that they don't have false hopes of achieving that term. This doesn't mean that you inform them of things you would not like to accept—only let them know of terms that are certain to be dealbreakers. Phrase it in a way that makes the other side hopeful that a positive, useful deal can be done, with the exclusion of that term. For example, one way to phrase a "bad news" statement might be, "I wanted to let you know that I cannot offer you more than twelve thousand dollars for a car, no matter what else we can come to terms on. I thought I should tell you that up front, so that you don't waste your time and I don't waste mine. But I'm willing to work with you to discuss the terms and options on any car under twelve thousand dollars." In this way, the relationship with the salesperson is preserved, even if you haven't given him news he wanted to hear.

During the negotiation you should listen carefully and take notes. If something they say doesn't immediately suggest to you a creative alternative, writing it down on paper will make it available for you to work with later. Also, taking notes offers you a great defense against any claims that you misinterpreted the other side's statements.

Some people believe in taping the negotiation to defend themselves against such misrepresentations. We are against videotaping or audiotaping your bargaining sessions. Taping a negotiation introduces a climate of suspicion and mistrust. But if the other side does it, a good defense is to bring a tape recorder of your own. You'll find that at first, both of you will be very careful and limited in what you say and how you act. Over time, however, as the deal demands it, you will offer creative alternatives, and the other side will consider options it didn't consider before the bargaining began. Eventually, you'll both stop taping the negotiation and get on with the deal.

You've got to be careful about how much you believe the other side. You have to separate the objective facts from the facts as presented by them. Are they going to lie to you? Most times, they won't. People tend to negotiate honestly, because if they are found out to be lying, they lose all credibility with the other party. But will most people misrepresent facts? Maybe, if it helps.

A good general rule to follow is: The more they pressure you with their facts, the more you should discount them. A smart way to defend against being pressured by facts is to come armed with your own. You can also parry the other side's facts by questioning how their set of numbers was reached. By digging into the foundation of any set of numbers you can find a host of information to discuss. Pay attention to where and how they get their facts—you may find a wealth of value hidden.

You have to pay attention to how someone presents those facts. Just because she prints sheets of information or provides you with manufacturer suggested prices, doesn't mean you have to take those as a final price. Don't give in to the Power of the Press. Before you step into the negotiation, it is important to adopt a position of benign skepticism. There is a world of difference between listening to what someone says and believing every word of it without question.

Making Concessions

The negotiation, however, doesn't always go the way you dream it will. Look at the following negotiation, in which each side has a set expectation of how the deal will eventually turn out.

"Tell me about this car."

"It's a 1995 Grenada Coupe, it gets great mileage, it comes with power steering, power windows, air conditioning, four-wheel drive, a ten-CD changer in the trunk, a four-year/100,000 mile warranty. It has custom colors such as metallic indigo and electric maroon, and it costs $17,541."

"It sounds great, but $17,541 sounds too much for me. I wanted to spend around $14,000. Is there any way you could move on that price?"

"No, not with those options."

"You see I want those options. I might be able to go with a common color, if it could bring down the price."

"I can give you $17,520 for a normal color."

"Yipes! Is that all?"

"That's what it costs."

"Well, if I agree to the price, what about warranty? Can I get an extra three years on it?"

"For an additional $600."

"You can't just throw it in?"

"I've got to price things based on their cost. The car is the car. It costs what it costs. I can give you a free gift certificate to the CD store around the corner for $25 if you buy the car."

"Fifty dollars would seem better. You can't even get two CDs these days for $25."

"The gift certificates are already made out. Why don't you get back to me when you make a decision?"

Don't expect the other side to fall down in front of you and give up everything you want just because you've done your homework. Negotiating is tough business, and as this example illustrates, some people are going to be tougher than others. As soon as the two of you begin to discuss terms, you are going to realize something— if you are expecting the other side to make concessions to you, you are going to have to make some concessions to them. Does this mean that all the preparation and anticipation you've done and all the skills you've learned are rendered useless? Of course not. All the pre-deal work you've done will help you minimize what you give up and maximize what you get.

If you can get away without conceding a thing, then by all means, sign that deal. After all, it's everything you wanted. But if the other side doesn't ask for a single thing, then you can be fairly certain that you could have asked for more and gotten it. Remember that maintaining a high valuation on your initial terms works to your advantage.

Most likely, they are going to ask you to concede something. When they do, defend your position. Explain to them how you arrived at the terms you did. Try moving to another topic before you agree to a concession—leave the topic open to further discussion. It is alright to intimate that you might be willing to make a concession on that term, but you want to see the deal as a whole first. It is important to have an understanding about the parameters of the entire deal before you make a decision on any single term. Remember—any single term is meaningless without looking at the context of the deal.

According to Mark McCormack, CEO of International Management Group, these are the most important attributes of a top negotiator:

1. *Doesn't have to be liked.*
2. *Tolerates ambiguity and conflict.*
3. *Doesn't have to be smarter than everyone else in the room.*
4. *Is willing to negotiate anything.*

Just because you are changing your understanding of how the deal will work—and are prepared to make some concessions—this doesn't mean that you assign less value to aspects of the deal. You will still aim high in what you desire to receive for your money and what terms you expect to get, but you will also be realistic. Let's look at that same car negotiation again, except this time the buyer has a more realistic understanding of the process. Note that he doesn't lower his standards at all—but he does alter his perception of the requirements of making a deal.

"Tell me about this car."

"It's a 1995 Grenada Coupe, it gets great mileage, it comes with power steering, power windows, air conditioning, four-wheel drive, a ten-CD changer in the trunk, a four-year/100,000 mile

warranty. It has such custom colors as metallic indigo and electric maroon, and it costs $17,541."

"It sounds great, but $17,541 sounds too much for me. I wanted to spend around $14,000. Is there any way you could move on that price?"

"No, not with those options."

"What's the most expensive option in the car?"

"Probably the power steering, but that's tough to take out."

"I want to keep that in anyway."

"You can save about $1,000 if you drop the power windows and the air conditioning."

"Well, I guess I could do that. But it still runs above my price range. What about the CD-changer?"

"That'd save you about $500. And I was supposed to offer you a $25 CD gift certificate, but since you won't be needing that, I'll take it off the bill."

"So it's down to around $16,000. If the price can't get any lower, what else can I get that makes this deal worthwhile?"

"What do you mean?"

"Do you offer any financing or insurance options? Do you have any demo or other models? Do you have anything that you can throw in to make this deal worth my while?"

"We offer good financing and we've got a preferred insurance dealer. Do you have a good driving record?"

"Clean as a whistle."

"Then we can save you around $300 a year on insurance. And if you take our insurance and financing, I can throw in an extra couple of years on the warranty for free."

"This is beginning to sound like a deal. Why don't we step into your office and talk about exact terms."

By asking questions and making concessions with the expectation of getting other concessions in return, this buyer and seller have both been working toward getting a deal done. Notice that the first option the dealer offers to drop, the purchaser concedes. This brings us to an important topic. How and when should you make concessions?

The size and speed with which you offer them transmits a message to the other side about your willingness to give up parts of the deal to get the deal done.

The first concession you make should be the largest one you are willing to give. This establishes a tone of openness and willingness to compromise. If you need to make any further concessions, make them smaller than your first one. Why? Because this gives the other side an important piece of information—that you are willing to give less and less as the negotiation goes on. Space your concessions out over a period of time. If you offer a flurry of concessions early in the negotiating process, and then offer nothing after that, you're transmitting two contradictory messages. You are giving one message that says you are willing to concede on a number of issues, then a second message that says you are unwilling to concede on any issue. Consistent message-sending is important. If the other side has an unrealistic view of what you will be willing to concede, you have to let them know right away that they must alter their perceptions. If you don't, they will continue discussing the deal with an attitude that leaves little room for negotiated compromise and creative alternatives. They will hardball you into concession after concession until you've given up everything to get the deal done.

Not only do you have to consider the size of a concession and the quickness with which you give it up, but you also have to consider how you give it up. If you give up anything without at least a small fight, you transmit a message that it was of little value to you. The other side thinks there must be more that you will be willing to give up. Even if the issue doesn't mean much to you, sigh and grunt a little. If they back off, you can always give it up later. If you are forced to concede it, you've made your point. It took some work on their part to get that from you—now they owe you something in return.

Unions and management in professional sports are extremely distrustful of each other, so much so that both sides usually delay substantive negotiations until weeks before existing deals expire. The result is that since 1973 there have been eight work stoppages in baseball, two work stoppages in the NFL, numerous basketball threats, and for an entire year before the owners locked the players out in 1994, hockey was played despite the lack of an agreement between players and owners. Maybe it's time for both sides to get some relationship therapy.

Never make a unilateral concession. If you give up something without asking for something in return, you're transmitting another message—that you are willing to give up parts of the deal regardless of the other side's willingness to give up parts of the deal. That message must be false if you intend to come out of the negotiation with anything close to fulfillment. If you are going to give up anything, give it up as part of a trade. After all, your contentment with the deal is being affected by having to make a concession on a term you assigned some value to. Try to find a number of places that are of value to you that the other side could compromise on. Don't make the mistake of linking forever two terms—you want to remain flexible on your responses to their offers. For example, saying, "I'll give in on price if you give in on volume," puts the other side in a very awkward position. The other side may be willing to give in on a number of terms, but by pigeonholing them into one term they must give in on, you limit their ability to respond to you. A much better way to phrase this might be, "If I lower the price, I'm going to need something back in return. I might be willing to give in on price if you increase your volume. Or, if volume is a problem, we can change the terms of payment. What can you offer that would give me a chance to lower my price?"

Usually, when you're at an impasse with another party, someone will suggest that the two of you "split the difference." What's wrong with splitting the difference? Plenty. You lose half as much as you wanted. If you can't find a creative way to get more value from the deal, then splitting means you both lose something. While it seems to be the most "fair" outcome, splitting the difference is actually just a way to avoid the work of negotiation.

Terms are only linked because an equitable tradeoff at that point can be reached. Once you've moved on to another set of concerns, those terms are always available for discussion. A deal is the sum of all its parts, and the true value of a deal cannot be determined until you've come to agreement on all of its terms.

> *Giving up concessions without asking for anything in return signals to the other side that there's more where that came from. The most famous instance of sending a chump-like message with your concessions came from Neville Chamberlin, Prime Minister of England, in the years prior to World War II. Chamberlin resorted to a "policy of appeasement" in which his response to Germany's seizure of Poland and Czechoslovakia was to try to establish peace without forcing Germany to relinquish this territory. The Germans, justifiably doubtful that England would change this policy, kept up a steady pace of invasions on neighboring countries. Only when France, the doormat of Europe, was invaded did England decide to change its policy and transmit a more resolute message to the German military.*

When making any kind of tradeoff, identifying the areas of value to the other side is very important. If you know what is valuable to them, you can find something to trade that is worth less to you. Then, you can trade this item of lower value for something they have that is valuable to you. By noting carefully the arguments they put forth for each topic, you can determine how much value they place on that item or term. What is their attitude toward this feature of the deal? Do they seem willing to discuss it at length? Do they seem agitated when you bring it up? Do they want to move on quickly to another topic and leave that issue unsettled for the time being? During the negotiation, use their reactions to let you know about the availability of a topic for discussion and its value as a potential concession. It may be helpful to think of a negotiation as a poker game—only you know what cards you hold and only you know what cards you need. By paying attention to how the other side reacts to their cards, you can gain important information on how strong they think their hand is.

Negotiating Workshop #12

Assigning Value and Trading

Read the scenario below, then assign a value to each item on the list. Then read the other party's scenario and assign a value for them on the same list. Identify the areas of potential swap benefits—where one party can trade an item of low value to the other party for an item of higher value.

Michael George is renegotiating his recording contract with Nosy Records. Mr. George is upset because in the past Nosy hasn't promoted his releases well, and his sales have suffered. Mr. George writes his own songs, and records most of his own music, but Nosy has the right to choose the producer for his CDs. He has had numerous artistic differences with the producers hired by Nosy which have resulted in large arguments and bad publicity. While many of the executives have been displeased with Mr. George's recordings over the years, nearly every one has been a commercial success. Mr. George feels that because most of his income results from the sale of his releases, Nosy's failure to promote him properly has hurt him in his bank account. Mr. George has some of the most popular videos in town and knows himself to be a marketable talent in the industry. If he doesn't reach an agreement with Nosy, however, he will have to go to court and can expect a legal battle that might continue for a number of years. Given the fleeting fame of musicians, a protracted legal battle could spell the end of his career.

The terms Mr. George has identified as being on the negotiating agenda are:

1. Money—how is he paid and how much?
2. Producers—who has control?
3. Promotion—how much and how often?
4. Term of Contract—years or number of releases?
5. Artistic Control—do the executives have it or does he?

Nosy Records has had a stormy relationship with Mr. George. While every release has been a success, that success was not immediately evident. Mr. George continues to change his style with every CD, and that makes it difficult for the promotion department—they don't know who to try to sell his CDs to! The largest problem for them, though, is the frequency of Mr. George's releases. Due to big (and public) spats with his producers over the years, Mr. George has always come out with his recordings late, nearly five months after a large campaign had been initiated. Nosy Records provides every artist with a talented producer—they are proud of this and don't understand why Mr. George has such trouble. While they have made a lot of money with Mr. George over the years, they have received a large amount of bad publicity which is making it difficult for them to attract new artists. If they do not reach an agreement with Mr. George, more bad publicity will result that could impact the company for a number of years. Additional loss of income to the company is a distinct possibility if they need to go to court and Mr. George refuses to record during that time.

Be Aware of Emotion

At the negotiating table, you're likely to encounter surprisingly bad behavior. People take negotiations personally and invest a lot of emotion and energy into them. Don't be surprised if people behave irrationally or don't seem to play by any logical set of rules. The most familiar example of an irrational negotiation emerges in a personal relationship. People have so much invested and so much history with each other that the negotiation is rarely about the purported topic.

> *"So I think California would be a great vacation."*
>
> *"You would! I think Florida would be much better."*
>
> *"But California has everything that Florida has—seafood, ocean, sun—and it has the wine region. We could drive down to Mexico, we could go hiking in the mountains—"*
>
> *"It's not Florida. I like the water in the Atlantic much better than the Pacific."*
>
> *"The water is just about the same."*
>
> *"Not true! You just don't want to go to Florida because I suggested it."*
>
> *"That's not true. I just think that California is like Florida plus more stuff. I think it'd make a better vacation spot."*
>
> *"I don't. I guess we have to agree to disagree."*

When the negotiation heads down a volatile and personal path, you have to find a way to steer it back to the issues at hand without aggravating the personal issues that are already at stake. Again, the use of the question is immensely valuable here. Use questions to open the discussion up.

"So I think California would be a great vacation."

"You would! I think Florida would be much better."

"But California has everything that Florida has—seafood, ocean, sun—and it has the wine region, we could drive down to Mexico, we could go hiking in the mountains—"

"It's not Florida. I like the water in the Atlantic much better than the Pacific."

"What do you like about the water?"

"It's not as salty."

"You don't like salty water?"

"No, not really."

"What do you want out of a vacation?"

"I don't know, sun, relaxation, some interesting things to see."

"How about Arizona? It's warm, there are fresh-water streams, there's the desert and Death Valley and all the spas out there."

"Sounds interesting."

By asking questions, one party opens up the discussion and can change the entire negotiating mindset. In emotional situations you have to acknowledge the emotional state of the other party. If you don't, you are going to run into the illogical negotiator problem, which almost always leads to the end of discussions.

Emotions shouldn't be simply dismissed—after all, even the person you're negotiating with is human. Take his feelings into consideration. Behave as if you want to make him comfortable. By thinking about the things that drive you crazy, you can avoid driving him crazy. Don't tap your foot or bite your pencil or clip your fingernails during the negotiation. These may seem hardly worth mentioning, but any generally annoying habit you have is going to work against you at the negotiating table. Before you walk into that room, think of all the things people have asked you to stop doing, from picking your nose to whistling in an elevator, and make sure you don't do them during the negotiation.

Silence is Golden

Try being comfortable with silence. People have a need to hear sound, and, if they are in a room with other people, to talk. Cubicles, which gained great popularity during the 1980s, were not only designed to give each worker some privacy, but also to discourage workers from talking with each other. Companies couldn't afford building each worker a separate office, so they decided to wall off each person from the others. Talking did decrease—it worked.

But, thankfully, you will never negotiate from cubicle to cubicle. When you are facing someone, you feel a desire to talk and to fill the empty space between you. Of all bad behavior, talking merely to fill the silence is the worst. Don't ever do it. Even if the silence is deafening, you have to learn to live with the silence after you've said what you intended to say. Don't ramble on if they don't respond right away. Let the other side fill the silence with their talk. Why should you use silence to your advantage? Three reasons:

1. Silence is unsettling. It makes people feel uneasy and unsure of their position. A little bit of silence after the other side has finished presenting their argument will undermine their sureness about their position.

2. Silence is interpreted negatively. The act of sitting across from the other person and saying nothing makes the other side feel their position has been received negatively. For some people, silence means the chance to negotiate is drawing to a close. Often, just remaining silent can make the other side immediately come up with another offer, one with better terms for you.

3. Silence can bring you information. Even if silence doesn't result in an immediately lower offer, the other side's desire to fill the silence may lead them to reveal information you can use during the negotiation. For

example, they may try to explain how they reached their figures. Never stop them from giving you more information about their pricing structure.

What if the other side is silent? That's wonderful. Just keep quiet and let the silence pass. If you have anything you should have said initially, by all means, bring it up, but don't expand on a topic unless they ask, don't justify your figures unless they ask, and don't modify your proposal unless they ask. If you are uncomfortable with the silence, ask a question of the other negotiator. But the best advice is to live with the silence.

Don't Bid Against Yourself

This discussion brings us to a crucial point. Never bid against yourself. This means that if another party turns down your initial offer, don't make another bid right away. Respond with questions to pinpoint what they are dissatisfied with. Explain to them the reasons for your terms. Try to get them to work with you and make a proposal to you about what they need to make the deal happen. Do not come back with another offer until you have had these discussions. If you bid once, and they turn you down, and then you bid again right away at more favorable terms for the other party, what message do you think you are transmitting to them? What do you think they will expect? They'll expect that if they turn you down again, you'll come back again with better terms. By involving them in the process and working together toward a deal, you get them to understand your limits, what you are prepared to do, and, more importantly, what you are *not* prepared to do. But bid against yourself and you'll end up frustrated, with a less fulfilling deal than you imagined.

Pleading Poverty

A good way to discourage parties from asking you to bid against yourself is to turn your pockets inside out and tell them that's all you have. The simple act of stating in a clear and straightforward way that you have no more money to spend can stop the most aggressive bargainer from expecting to get any more from your side in a deal. Also, it keeps communication fresh and lively. You can always sympathize with the other side by saying that you wish you had more money, or that if you had more money you'd offer it for their product or services, but you simply don't have it. Sometimes, this can be the kick that startles the other side into getting to a deal on your terms.

Mediation

Sometimes a troublesome negotiation can he helped by bringing in a third party, a mediator, to help both sides come to an agreement. The mediator doesn't choose one side over the other or make any decisions that both sides have to agree to—that's called arbitration, and is usually the last step before litigation. The mediator isolates the issues and provides a framework so that the negotiations can move forward. You might want to consider using a mediator when the other side is not focusing on the issues that need to be discussed, when a personality conflict is affecting your discussion, or when both sides feel lost in all the details of a complicated deal. A mediator can get messy negotiations back on track without making either side feel that they've been manipulated.

Although the story was later denied, The Sun reported a three-way deal that had Mobil Oil paying American Poultry to deliver 528 million pounds of chicken legs to the Russian Ministry of Food in exchange for oil development rights in Russia. The deal fell through, saving one billion chickens from a legless fate.

Be Willing to Walk

If your discussions of the terms go poorly, you have one final alternative to avail yourself of. Walk away from the deal. If you cannot picture making a deal with that company or salesperson, walk away. If you cannot live with the final terms the other side presents, walk away. Don't create bad will and huff and storm away from the negotiation table. Don't yell at the salesperson who won't give you a better price. Make clear your reasons for leaving and keep the possibility of another deal in the future open. Walking away with dignity and a clear understanding of why the deal failed only helps you in future negotiations, both in terms of information and in terms

of the relationship with the other party. And you might be surprised—
the other party may catch you at the door, more willing to be flexible
on the terms they proposed.

The Power of the Penalty

It is common to include in any agreement a penalty clause stating
what punishment each side suffers in the event of non-compliance
with the agreement. In a car purchase, it usually takes the form of
an agreement to provide a substitute car if a new car needs any repair
work. In a supplier relationship, it can take the form of a discount
on price for late delivery or a cash penalty for non-delivery. Think
carefully about inserting a penalty clause, because once you've brought
up the idea, the other side is certain to want one too. If you do
want one, insert a fair and reasonable clause for each term and be
prepared to accept the same for you. Don't attempt to impose a huge
and burdensome penalty on the other side for a minor infraction.
For example, if a car is delivered a day late to your doorstep, don't
ask for another car free. It will hurt your credibility, and the other
side will be annoyed at your lack of rationality.

---

*I called a credit card company the other day to let them
know I thought their rates were too high and to ask if they
had any cards with lower rates. Before I could get to my
second sentence, the man on the other end said "I can
lower your rate in half for six months, and if that's not
enough, I'll see what else I can do." Of course, I responded that that wasn't enough. I wanted to see what
else they could do. This exchange illustrates two crucial
points. First, if you're dissatisfied with something, don't
be afraid to ask for more. Remember you get what you
settle for in life. Second, note what a bonehead the credit
card company rep was. Before I could even respond to
his offer, he told me he'd be willing to make an even
better one.*

If you've come to a point in the negotiating session when both
sides are close to a deal but some self-imposed deadline has been
reached, don't be afraid to extend the deadline. Any deadline, unless

it relies on other parties, can be extended. Deadlines are useful in order to get both sides to negotiate and to assign a level of seriousness to the discussions. Once you've got both sides committed to the negotiation, deadlines aren't as important as progress.

Ask for a "Tip"

Toward the end of a deal, there is one negotiating tactic that you should always try. It doesn't significantly affect good will, and, over a number of negotiations, the more you use it the more fulfillment you are going to have. You should always ask for a "tip" as a way of bringing a deal to a close. A tip is a small item of little value to the other side that will make you want to agree to the deal. Picture the deal as a balanced scale that can go in either direction. The tip will "tip" the deal to the side of getting done. It should be something that you are fairly certain the other side will be willing to part with. Don't make it a "make or break" term. If the other side refuses the tip, then fine, you asked for it and didn't get it. You gave it a shot. If you get it, then you have one more reason to finish the deal. A good way to phrase a request for a tip is something like this:

"You know what would make this deal easier to get done quickly? If we can change the terms of payment from net 35 days to net 30 days. I know it's not much, but my boss really likes deals with net 30 day terms, and he's more likely to deal with this contract quickly if it's net 30 days."

Or like this: "I think we can finish this deal today, if you'll throw in that speaker wire and those stereo connectors with the price of the stereo. I'd love to take this system home this afternoon."

Remember—when you ask for a tip, don't ask for anything big. Don't threaten the deal with it—make it known that to give you this tip would hasten and conclude your dealings. Keep in mind another meaning of "tip": In a restaurant, you leave a tip to encourage prompt and attentive service. In a deal, the tip should function in the same general way. Make sure that your request for a tip is understood by the other side as just that—just a tip—and not a demand that would cause the deal to fall apart if not met. If the other side asks for a tip in return, take your time. Place a value on the tip they ask for. If the stereo salesperson asks you to purchase a store warranty with your stereo in return for the speaker wire and connectors, compare the worths of the tips. You may be saving ten dollars and getting an additional two years of service. For the salesperson, he's getting a tiny commission on speaker wire and connectors but a large commission on the store warranty, so he assigns more value to that than you do. Especially in the realm of tips, differences in assigning value come to light and should be taken into account.

When a Deal is a Deal

A deal isn't a deal until it's done. Don't rush to a conclusion when things start moving ahead. We've talked about how you're right to revisit terms until you've had a chance to review the deal on the whole and assess its fulfillment level to you. Keep that squarely in mind. We recommend that you explain to the other side before you begin the negotiation that you want to discuss each part and term of the contract, but that you'll have to review the agreement as a whole once you've come to a preliminary agreement on some terms. At that point, if the deal does not satisfy you, you have no obligation to agree to it.

When is a deal done? When you've come to mutually agreed-upon terms and both parties state explicitly that the terms are acceptable, then you have a deal. Commonly, once the two of you shake hands, it's over. If something unusual or critical happens between the time you shook hands and the time the deal gets signed, make sure to explain that event to the other side before you ask them to reopen negotiations. There is nothing that erodes good will more than reopening a closed negotiation. Once you've signed the deal, however, that negotiation is closed. If you want to reopen it at any time, then a new negotiation has begun.

The negotiation should be intense, thoughtful, and exciting. You may even find it fun. Remember, you have a warehouse full of skills and information that the other side might not have.

CHAPTER 8

Post-Negotiation Strategies

When the deal is done, your work isn't over. Much as you think the negotiations have been concluded, remember—most negotiations are part of a larger, longer term relationship. And even if you're certain you'll never see the other party again, there's still some work to take care of.

The first thing you should do once a deal has concluded is to carefully examine the document you are asked to sign. Make certain that all the terms in the contract are exactly what you perceived them to be during the negotiation. You never want to accuse the other side of trying to alter the terms of the deal without your knowing— but any time you sign a legally binding piece of paper, you want to make sure you understand in great detail what is on it.

PLAY "JEOPARDY" WITH YOUR PROBLEMS

If you find any discrepancies between what you negotiated and the contract you are asked to sign, or any clauses you don't understand, bring them up in the form of a question. Let the other side explain how they reached that clause, detail or phrasing. Most often, a small misunderstanding can be taken care of by a minor adjustment on the spot. If the other side has any questions, however, do not respond to them as insignificant. Treat them with care and in detail. If you afford their questions respect, they will treat your questions in a similarly serious manner. If you still feel your questions haven't been properly answered, arrange a face-to-face meeting where you once again let the other side know your needs. Take time to make sure you grasp what you are about to sign. Once you've signed a deal, you're pretty much stuck with it, unless you want to plunge into litigation (discussed later in this chapter).

Monitor the deal as it takes place. Are the terms of the deal being obeyed? Is the other person doing what she's supposed to be doing when she's supposed to be doing it? If the other side isn't fulfilling her obligations, then you're going to have to try to enforce any penalties you negotiated into the contract. As in a negotiation, there's a right and a wrong way to communicate this failure of performance to the other side. Without the communication skills you learned earlier, you might have enforced an overdue contract like this:

> *"Hey Jonny—I just got this letter in the mail from your lawyer that we owe you $600?"*
>
> *"Yeah, Steve."*
>
> *"What is this? We had a deal!"*
>
> *"Yeah, and your trucks were three days late. In the deal we made an agreement. For every day late that materials arrive, the supplier will be charged $200."*
>
> *"You never told me you needed them right away. I would've hired extra trucks."*
>
> *"Read the contract next time. It says it right on page 12."*

By sticking to the contract, Jonny is clearly in the right. Steve cannot argue against the contract. But how easy do you think it is to get payment from someone who is unhappy with the way things turned out and feels the other side failed him in terms of communicating their need? By using some of the skills taught earlier, enforcement of existing agreements becomes much more pleasant. Let's look at the same discussion with a true negotiator who's realized his job isn't over, even after the contract has been signed.

> *"Jonny, this is Steve. You called?"*
>
> *"Steve. Thanks for calling back. I'm calling to tell you about some trouble we had with your last shipment."*
>
> *"The quality was good, wasn't it?"*

"The quality was excellent. I have no problem with the quality. What I have a problem with was the timing. Your shipment was three days late."

"I didn't know you needed it right away."

"Just to let you know, I don't keep any raw materials inventory on my plant site. So every day your truck doesn't show up, I have to go out and buy materials somewhere else to keep things running."

"I'm sorry. I didn't know. I had some drivers out with the flu and I thought I'd just wait until they got better."

"Well, I managed to get some elsewhere, but it cost me some money. More money than it would have cost if your stuff had been here."

"You should have called me. I would have hired extra drivers."

"You can keep this as a standing note—when we have a date on a delivery, I need it that date or I have to shut down."

"I will, Steve."

"But about those expenses. I'm going to have to enforce the on-time delivery clause in the contract because of the money I lost on materials. But now that we've cleared up this delivery problem, I don't expect to ever have to do it again."

"No, now that I know your production needs, I can get the materials to you on time."

"Great. I love the quality of the last shipment. Keep it coming."

"Except on time."

"Except on time."

Steve has a much better understanding of why on-time delivery is important, and he is more likely to see the importance in maintaining an on-time delivery record once he understands that Jonny is relying on his materials. Also, since Jonny does choose to enforce the contract, he transmits a clear message to Steve. Jonny is willing to enforce the contract and make Steve pay for his non-performance. You send signals with your enforcement (or your lack of enforcement) of the penalty clauses in any agreement.

Monitoring the performance of the other party is critical to your future negotiations. By keeping accurate track of the other party's actions, you gain useful information for the next set of discussions.

For example, if the other party delivers goods late on four separate occasions, do you think that might help you in your next bargaining session? Of course it will. Once you have this important piece of information, you can use it as a bargaining chip during your discussions. You can choose to negotiate the price of the goods, or you can negotiate a more strict on-time delivery clause, whichever is more important to you. Having ammunition like a poor delivery record lets you dictate more of the terms of the next contract negotiation. What if the other side never delivers any goods late? That too will help you. You can expect that they will emphasize their excellent service record. By focusing your arguments on the other aspects of the product and dismissing on-time delivery as normal behavior, you will manage to keep them from using their spotless record to demand more concessions from you. Keeping track of the other party's actions is critical to any ongoing relationship.

If you've signed a contract in a competitive field, keep track of prices in the market. Continue to meet with other suppliers and get their best offers, even if your contract is not set to expire for some time. Don't lie to competitive bidders and tell them that you are going to sign a contract with them imminently, but let them know that you are always on the lookout for an aggressive company that can consistently deliver quality. Do research into the performance records of other companies. The more weapons you can arm yourself with for the next deal, the better off you are going to be. If your supplier hears that you've been shopping around for a better supply contract, most likely they're going to contact you and see if they can do anything to keep you as a purchaser. By simply checking the market, you can expect better terms on your next deal. As well, the current supplier will be very careful about performing to the letter of your contract. You can cut down on delays or non-payment simply by letting it be known that you are ready to listen to anyone with a good offer.

Negotiating Workshop #13

Keeping on Top

On the list below, identify the situations in which you would continue to check prices in the market.

1. You have just purchased a new car.
2. You have just purchased a used car.
3. You have just bought a piece of art at an auction.
4. You have just signed a lease with a new landlord.
5. You have just signed a deal with an office supply contractor.
6. You have just sold your house.
7. You have just agreed to have an addition built on your house.
8. You have just bought a stock.
9. You have just purchased a service contract with a copier-repair firm.
10. You have just purchased a new suit.

> *New situations can make unexpected alliances. Check out these strange bedfellows: the meatpackers union and the FDA allied against the Heart Association's request for meat labeling; the appliance industries and certain environmental groups banded together against the EPA's proposed changes in effluent waste standards; and the chemical industry and the EPA united against the environmentalist groups who demanded extremely strict chemical standards. Never be afraid to approach former antagonists and make them your allies, if the cause is right.*

If you have purchased something, like a stereo or a car, and you find that the dealer's promises have not lived up to the performance, it's a good idea to let the other side know of your dissatisfaction. If the car is continually in the auto-repair shop or the stereo is always on the fritz, make sure that your salesperson knows of your unhappiness. Transmit an unwavering message that you are displeased with the product and that the salesperson's promises didn't live up to your expectations. Usually, the salesperson will do everything she can do to maintain your fulfillment with the product by offering extra warranties, loaner cars, replacements, or substitutions. Much consumer unhappiness stems from not clearly informing the salesperson about problems with the product. Positive responses by the salesperson are not uncommon for those consumers who take the time to make their unpleasant experiences known. Here, above all else, show a willingness to complain to someone in higher authority than your salesperson, preferably her boss. This will push your salesperson to do everything she can. There is nothing worse for a salesperson than for a customer to complain to a supervisor, particularly if the customer is complaining that the salesperson didn't follow through on her promises. Stores trade not only on their products but on their reputations. Any salesperson who jeopardizes a store's reputation is going to be in trouble.

> *Victor Kiam, owner of the New England Patriots, has a slogan about his electric razor company. "I liked the product so much I bought the company." His other slogan is "Shaves as close as a blade or your money back." Kiam's focus on his product's reputation gives him an edge on the competition in any negotiation—his guarantees give him a trustworthy aura that is always an advantage.*

Keep track of the market for new opportunities to revisit and revise your contract. For example, if you are supplying gumdrops to a candy store and there is an article on how gumdrops prevent heart attacks in your local paper, you may want to revisit that contract and, after bringing the article to the store's attention, ask if they want to increase the volume of their purchase. Bringing additional information to the other party after the contract is complete can work to your advantage. At the same time, if you know that the person you sold a car to has been hired by a major executive service firm, you may want to arrange a meeting with him to discuss potential corporate contracts that he may be in a position to offer. Keep track of the fortunes of people or companies you have negotiated a contract with. The more you know about their position and obligations, the more likely you are to suggest useful renewals or expansions of that relationship. Potential opportunities for new deals often arise from old business relationships. One feature of the good negotiator is the recognition that people's and companies' needs change over time, and the business that is most responsive to those changes will keep clients. Never discount potential opportunities from old contracts and old contractors. Is this part of a negotiation? Yes. Maintaining a long-term relationship is the purpose and result of every good negotiation.

For example, one real estate broker from the William B. May real estate company in New York sends New Year's cards to his clients every year. In the cards he informs them of any address or telephone number changes in case they wish to get in touch with him and describes a couple of apartments that he has available at the time. Aside from the fact that he provides quality apartments, it is significant that he doesn't abandon his clients once they have chosen an apartment. Since the average tenure in a New York apartment is 3.4 years, he is being smart about his negotiations. Once a year he reminds people of the good apartment he got for them and that he is available if they are looking for another apartments in the same neighborhood. Most of his clients, not surprisingly, come to him as a result of recommendations from other clients. Much of his business, again not surprisingly, is return business. Through his actions after the negotiations, he manages to maintain his reputation and encourage further deals.

Once you conclude the negotiation, it is also important to keep in mind what *not* to do. Avoid discussing the concluded negotiation and particularly avoid speculating with the other party about "what might have been." You'd be surprised at how many negotiations initially fulfill both parties, yet eventually fail the satisfaction test because of what is said after the negotiations are done. Speculation only informs the other party of all the things they didn't get. For example, Linda and Maria are sitting at dinner, one day after they've signed a multi-million dollar contract with each other.

"You know, Linda, I'm glad that's over."

"So am I Maria. You were tough on price and payment. But I got you on length of contract."

"What do you mean?"

"You wanted three years, I wanted one, we settled on two. I was willing to go to four years, if I had to."

"I would have loved four years. That would have made the deal great for me."

"Too bad."

"If you would have given me four years, I would have caved in on price and payment."

"What?"

"Oh yeah. I could have cut fifteen percent off the price."

"FIFTEEN PERCENT?"

"Too bad, I guess."

How do you think this new information has affected the negotiation? While both sides were happy with the deal before, they now both feel dissatisfaction with all that they didn't know they could have gotten. Just as significant, they each feel upset with their performance as a negotiator. It is important to understand that in any deal you spend time and energy on, it is impossible to completely divorce your ego from the results. Satisfy yourself with the understanding that in any good deal, there will be items both sides leave on the table. In many ways, that's the hallmark of a good negotiation. In other words, live with it. Don't let yourself become obsessed with what you didn't get.

There is another downside associated with post-deal chatting. How do you think this new information will affect the next negotiation? Both sides are going to aggressively pursue the terms the other said that they would have given in on if forced. Both sides, as well, are not going to be flexible. They will be single-minded in pursuit of those things they didn't get last time. Discussing terms and playing "what if" after the negotiation concludes puts barriers in the way of any future, productive, flexible negotiation.

Our final word on post-deal etiquette concerns litigation. As Donald Fehr, president of the Players Association for Major League Baseball, once said, "The talks have broken down. The discussions now move from the sphere of negotiation to one of litigation." Litigation is usually the result of a failed negotiation. If terms were not spelled out clearly, if one side has a notably different interpretation of a clause, or if one side refuses to recognize its obligation, then the discussions are likely to end in litigation. Most of the time litigation results from a failure in communication.

Litigation is useful as a threat, if you are in a very specific situation:

1. You do not care about your future relationship with the other party. Litigation is messy, offensive, time-consuming, and expensive. Litigation destroys all good will you've accrued to this point. Only when you have no other available options to enforce an existing contract should you consider litigation.

2. You have more time and financial resources available than the other side. If you are going to threaten liti-

gation, it is intended to bring the other side to an agreement quickly if one is possible. Litigation always favors the party with more money and more time. It will not be a useful threat if the other side knows that litigation will hurt your position more than it will hurt theirs.

3. You feel that there is at least a fifty percent chance that you will succeed in the litigation. If the other side is convinced that they would stand a better-than-fair chance of succeeding in litigation, they may not be as worried about the possibility as you'd like them to be.

Litigation is more useful as a threat, however, than an enforcement alternative, since it's not always successful, even when you believe you're in the right. It is an expensive gamble. The threat of litigation is a last resort only to be used in certain circumstances, and not to be taken lightly. Sometimes, the mere discussion of litigation can spark a new round of discussions and a flurry of creative alternatives.

In 1994, after a year-long strike, the Typographical Union at the Chicago Sun-Times tried to jump-start stalled negotiations by filing an age discrimination suit against the paper. Their reasoning was that fear of potential losses if the suit was successful would prod management back to the negotiating table. "It's a clever strategy, it's novel—and it doesn't have a snowball's chance in hell," said one labor lawyer. Use litigation to encourage negotiation only if you've exhausted all other options.

The importance of maintaining contact with your partners after a deal is concluded cannot be swept aside. You have to keep track of the market, keep an eye on the deal, and revisit the contract if situations require it. In many ways, you have more work to do after the negotiation than you do during it, however much it's worth the energy. By keeping attentive to the relationship created by your agreement, you increase the chance of future deals.

CHAPTER 9

The "X" Files

While you now have strength, skills, and surety going for you in your negotiations, there are still some situations that fall outside the realm of normal negotiations. These are the unusual negotiation situations, or as we like to call them, the "X"-Files (no disrespect intended to Fox Television, Rupert Murdoch, or David Duchovney), where only an unusual response can work to your advantage. These situations occur frequently enough to mention but require you to behave contrary to your normal reactions. So we've tailored the responses to these very specific instances. Take note—these situations are the exception and not the rule, so the solutions we propose are only useful in these situations. But, if you find yourself in an unusual situation where you think you have no power at all, you'll discover some great ways to take control of a negotiation using the following techniques.

X-File #1

Powerful Players

Certain bargaining sessions may arise in which you are negotiating with a person or a company that clearly has more power over the negotiation than you do. This situation may occur when you are renting an apartment from a large managing agent who rents thousands of apartments, when you are negotiating a first contract with a large corporation that has no reason to take you over any other competitive bidder, or when you are negotiating with a national chain or franchise that has a standard or set contract that they rarely deviate from. You feel that no matter how well you prepare and what you know about the other party, you can gain no advantage from that preparation. The other side appears to hold all the cards and you appear to hold none. It seems impossible to emerge from this negotiation with any degree of fulfillment.

Don't despair. You have options available to you. You just have to get in touch with your negotiating magic to be able to turn your cards from a pair of twos to a full house. Here's what you need to know:

Have No Fear

Negotiators can smell fear in the same way that animals can. The other side may come to the table with the idea that since their position is a strong one, they can intimidate you into accepting it with no input from you. If you approach the negotiation in a fearful manner, don't be surprised at the result. You must banish all qualms from your mind. Approach the negotiation with confidence and the honest understanding that if a large corporation is successful, it is based at least partially on a history of good relationships with all its various clients, vendors, and suppliers. Any relationship relies upon both sides coming to terms of agreement. Keep in mind that without you, there's no deal.

Argue Your Merits

If the other side tries to undermine your value to them, don't counter-attack. The other side knows the power they wield during the negotiation, and they won't lose any time trying to remind you of it. They are waiting for you to try to defend your position in the deal. Letting them draw you into a conflict over who is bringing more to the bargaining table is asking for defeat. Don't play their game—let them press their advantage and enumerate all their strengths. If you don't let it affect your underlying understanding of how negotiations work, then their attacks have no effect. Argue your merits rather than the other side's shortfalls. Use their comments as opportunities to point out where they can afford to make concessions while at the same time acknowledging their strengths. There's a hidden treasure of information buried in their comments. Read the following exchange and see how the "powerless" party manages to get the most out of her bargaining time:

"You know, there are a hundred computer companies we could get to do our inventory processing. Your proposal sounded interesting so we decided to bring you in. But we can't agree to your price structure and your overtime requests. If you can drop the price and get rid of the overtime altogether, we can make a deal. We service over three thousand clients a year, and we have to be there for them if they need our services. Otherwise we lose our reputation. If we factor in the overtime you requested, rather than being one of the lowest bidders, you turn into one of the highest bidders. Our reputation is important and we have thousands of clients we are responsible to. So let's talk about price."

"We've heard of your reputation in the industry, and that's one of the main reasons we wanted to send you a proposal. Your reputation is immaculate. Your clients are satisfied, and as to the hundred computer companies you could get in do your inventory, you are right. There are a hundred firms that are capable of trying to handle your inventory processing. What we bring is the same reputation in our field that you have in your field. We stand by our product one hundred percent. And that's why we included the potential overtime costs in our contract. We didn't want to tell you that in all circumstances you would be paying nearly nothing. If your needs exceed a certain level, we have to hire, train, and supervise extra people. We guarantee that your clients will not be left for a single minute without support and expert inventory processing. With us, your reputation is safe. Have you ever had an instance when you've been let down by one of your vendors?"

"Yes, and it was a disaster. We had to go out in the market, get the product ourselves, and eat a huge cost increase."

"That would never happen working with us. If we need anything to take care of your account, we pay for it, not you. And with our twenty-four-hour monitoring, not a single minute is wasted in having your control system down."

"I see why the overtime might be defensible, but we've had lower bids on price, and we need to get those down, otherwise I can't do this deal."

"We can discuss price, but I want to let you know exactly what that price includes. We have some special features that other companies don't offer. You may not care about these features now, but if you need them, you'll be very glad you had them..."

Do you see how the vendor isn't arguing the value or strength of the other side's position, but instead turning the focus of the discussion to the merits of her own product? There may be a hundred companies in that industry that have good reputations, but by listening to how much one side cares about an issue, this vendor managed to emphasize that aspect of her own company. Pick your fights carefully—argue positively.

Disappear

Point out the problem, then disappear. By "disappear," we mean that you should make the problem—not you—the focus of everyone's attention. For representatives of the United Nations, this method is critical to successful negotiations. Often, you can see the representatives from the two troubled countries sitting in the antechamber, sipping coffee and chatting while momentous and emotional issues are negotiated. The issues have taken center stage and the people have effectively disappeared. When you disappear, your magic begins to take effect. The energy the other side spends attacking you can be used to your advantage. Try to refocus the other side on the problem rather than on you. When the other side denigrates the value you bring to the deal, turn their attention to the problem in the contract they propose. Once the other side becomes engaged with the problem in the contract, they become a partner rather than an adversary. You "disappear" as a target and the problem itself becomes a target. This requires a delicate touch. You must readjust the other side's focus without making it apparent that you are stepping out of the way. A good idea is to begin by going over the other side's terms point by point and having the person explain how they reached those terms. As the person spends more and more time talking about his company and his set of concerns, then you can step in with creative alternatives. By helping

him get what he needs, you make an ally out of him and
you encourage him to deal with the problem rather than
blindly attacking your position.

Use Silence

Don't assume that you have to make all the suggestions
and the concessions. Particularly when you are involved
in a negotiation in which the other side has more strength
and positional advantage, silence can help you get stealth
concessions from the other side. By letting the other side
talk, you gain more information and turn the pressure on
them to find a solution. The best thing you can do is
encourage the other negotiator to be creative in solving
his own problems. Then the other party feels that he has
taken control of the negotiation and is likely to be more
generous in future concessions. Use silence when you are
clearly outmatched to drag the other party into a discussion
of terms.

By using this negotiating magic, you will find that the unusual
situation of negotiating with a more powerful party can turn into
one in which you too wield a great amount of power.

X-File #2

The New Negotiation

Negotiating initial contracts or agreements with a firm or person you
have never dealt with before should be treated very gingerly. Beginning
a relationship calls for extra sensitivity, because both sides are getting
to know each other. Expect the best but prepare for the worst. Most
people are more concerned with the second negotiation; they are
willing to make whatever concessions are needed to get the initial
account. But think for a minute: What kind of message are you sending
to your negotiating partners? Do you think they are going to expect
a change between the first and second negotiation? Do you think
they will be suddenly willing to make large concessions based on
the initial contract they signed? You have transmitted a message to

the other side with your first negotiation. You are going to have to live with the legacy of your first negotiation.

An initial deal can be negotiated on unusual terms if that is the only way it can be struck, but during that negotiation, it is your responsibility to make it clear that in the future, new terms will be considered. For example, most credit card companies offer an introductory rate as low as five-and-a-half percent for the first year for new customers. They write in fine print, however, that after that first year, the card reverts to a much higher rate, sometimes as high as twenty-one percent or more. If you can, you should avoid making initial concessions to the other side without linking some future behavior to it. One tool some people use to ensure that the other side knows of these term changes is to include a second contract that either side has a right to renew when the first one expires. This second contract can provide the framework for future negotiations, even if neither side chooses to activate that second contract. The most common example of this type of clause is an "option-year" in professional sports where the team owner can keep the services of a player for a pre-determined price after the regular term of his contract has expired. "Option-year" arrangements and those like them tend to keep negotiations open and friendly.

Steven Bochco, creator of "Cop Rock," "Hill Street Blues," and most recently "NYPD Blue," negotiated an odd agreement that allowed him to make "NYPD Blue" one of the most risqué shows in network TV history. He got ABC to allow partial nudity and a purported list of words that includes "mother jumper," "hump head," and other creative, semi-vulgar neologisms.

You also can't be afraid to be firm and direct in what you need and what you are willing to give up. Be forthright in setting your parameters for the initial negotiation. Be honest with yourself about the likelihood that the other party will terminate the negotiation and find another company—you don't want to shoot yourself in the foot. But in a new relationship, surprises can hurt you most. You don't want to raise the other side's expectations higher than you can deliver. Adjust your attitude so that it's straightforward and positive about your chances with the new company. Letting them dictate the terms of a first contract works to no one's advantage.

The last thing you need to do is adjust your understanding of how an initial negotiation takes place. Just because a negotiation is hard fought doesn't mean that the other side will be less likely to consider you if you state your needs and propose strong, highly valued positions. In any initial deal, both sides have a large amount of information to convey and a great deal of communication to attend to.

If any problems result, a good question to ask yourself is, "Have we dived into the details too early?" If you find yourself locked in position where the other side seems to disregard your need in a particular area, perhaps you should strive to use more Strategic Education. Or perhaps you need to seek more information from the other party. In a new negotiation, you want to be an active information seeker. Before the negotiation, you should make a list of all the things you need to know. Don't be limited to that list, however. Take your cues from the answers they give. You can never be too informed when it comes to a new client.

X-File #3

Negotiating With Friends

When you approach a friend or a friend approaches you about beginning a business relationship, there's a lot you will end up having to negotiate. Working with a friend or relative can be one of the most productive and personally rewarding things you do. It seems that it should do nothing but help your relationship, provide you with another layer of support, and financially reward you. But it can also be a nightmare. Like a purely professional relationship, the positive personal/business relationship only results from knowing how to negotiate with friends.

A good example of the problems lurking in any venture you enter into with friends occurred on the television show "Roseanne" from 1992 to 1994. At the beginning of 1992, Roseanne had bought a restaurant with her mother, her sister, and a friend, Nancy. The four went into the venture with only a verbal contract and with no agreement on how the business would be structured. They said they'd work out problems as they came up. By the end of the 1994 season, Roseanne had had over fifty fights with her co-owners about how to run the restaurant. Meanwhile, her mother had sold her portion of the business to a man named Leon, who subsequently schemed to buy everyone out and run the restaurant himself. While sitcoms are a far cry from real life, trust us—this restaurant deal would have blown up even sooner than "Roseanne" would have it. In real life, the friends/co-owners would most likely have ended up in court, suing each other for everything they could think of.

People tend to assume that because they have a personal relationship with another party, a business arrangement can be struck on better terms than would otherwise be possible. In some ways, many of the pre-negotiating ordeals are taken care of by knowing the other party. You have some good will accrued, you have an understanding of the other side's history, and you have already established a manner of communication that is helpful to both sides. However, everything that works for you can also work against you. The other side may know your needs more intimately than you would like. The other side may know what is important to you and how to use that to their best advantage. In many ways, the informational problems presented by a negotiation between friends may outweigh the informational problems prevented by knowing each other already. But equally important are the expectations of both parties. Each one is looking for a better deal than the market would provide. Can this happen? Sure, but the usual way that creative, win-win solutions occur is through flexible, creative and comprehensive negotiations, whether you've been friends for years or not.

On a professional level, you can't afford to choose one set of standards for deals with friends and another set of standards for your non-personal deals. You may move more quickly to creative alternatives and to compromise offers with a friend, but if you offer a deal that clearly favors the other party, you're worse off than if you got a new client through the mail. Soon, you'll begin to resent the whole situation, since you are spending the same amount of effort to achieve less fulfillment. Eventually, that dissatisfaction will resonate throughout the relationship.

What advantage you do have, though, emerges through your knowledge of the parties involved and your ability to make an informed judgment about what you understand the other side's level of reliability to be. This will help determine how strongly you should argue for enforcement clauses, timing issues, and accountability levels that you otherwise could only guess at.

Set down your terms up front and make things as clear as possible. Let the other side know that you value your relationship with them, but that you also value your business, just as they value theirs. The best way for both of you to stay satisfied is to reinforce the value of all three of those things, and the best way to manage that is through comprehensive negotiation. Communicate to them that they should welcome these negotiations and, in the same way, that neither one of you should expect a free ride.

A common mistake for friendly negotiators is to begin the negotiation in an inappropriate setting. Often one party will recommend that terms be discussed over dinner, or over drinks, or at one party's home. While these locations may be familiar and cordial, they are not good negotiating locations. Try to set up the negotiation in a place that is professional and appropriate. Unprofessional locations can lead to unprofessional conduct by both parties. Don't assume that you can be as articulate, as sharp, and as forceful with a plate of linguini in front of you or after two or three drinks as you would in a conference room with a pad full of notes in front of you. There's plenty of time to celebrate after the deal is done.

Diaz Dennis is a labor lawyer who once had to negotiate with a group of inmates at Folsom Prison who had been used as extras in an ABC movie and demanded more than SAG minimum. Mostly, she realized, they wanted the chance to leave the prison to negotiate. She didn't budge on their demands, but the negotiating sessions gave them a chance to break the monotony of prison life.

In a negotiation, there are going to be topics and subjects that you and the other side disagree upon. In the negotiation with a friend, you can use your relationship as a springboard to broach any difficult subject. Don't expect the other side to give in merely because you invoke the relationship, but nonetheless your affiliation should provide you with a way to open discussions on a topic without engendering ill will. For example, if one topic you need to discuss is a strict enforcement of terms of payment (if the other side doesn't pay within thirty days you want strict penalties), you can use your history together to broach the subject and to not accuse the other side of any bad motivations. You might say, "Look Barry, I'm sure you understand the needs of proper payment. I know how mad you were when Catalan Associates were behind on their payments every month. And I know that you'll never stiff me, and I'll never default on a delivery. So why don't we just put it in the contract? I guarantee that I give you delivery of the product or I pay a bunch, and you guarantee that you'll pay me in a timely fashion, or you pay me a bunch. I just want both of us protected here." A simple mention of a past understanding that didn't have this clause in it, as well as an affirmation that both parties want the best for the agreement, can smooth the way for the discussion of a potentially sticky subject.

You want to avoid as many tactics as possible in a personal negotiation. When you are trying to construct a deal with a friend or relative, you can only encourage ill will if you try to trick or over-technique the other party. Use the base of communication you have already established and be as forthright as possible. Trying out a tactic can easily blow up in your face.

One final note about failed attempts at negotiating a personal deal—if you can't make a deal, then you should make an effort to re-establish the relationship that existed before the business negotiation began. Even a failed deal should work to make both parties understand each other better. Make explicit the terms that prevented you from reaching a deal, then agree upon a plan to enjoy some non-business-oriented meeting soon after. By pointing out that at that time no deal was the best deal, you encourage the relationship while putting the negotiation in proper perspective.

X-File #4

The Rapid Negotiation

Occasionally, situations will arise that require rapid dealmaking. Unusual windows of opportunity present themselves, and you have to act quickly in order to take advantage of them. The first thing you must consider is—does this really have to be done right away? Often people merely prefer a fast negotiation, while in reality, the deal could take as much time as it needs. Determine if the opportunity will in fact not be available if you hesitate or delay the negotiations. Is this a matter of regulatory timing (for example, does it have to be done before the end of the year for tax reporting purposes)? Is this a result of a unique situation (for example, is there an extreme demand for your product immediately, like a fad or national interest)? Is the other side only going to test the waters for a brief period of time, and if they don't reach an agreement with you, will they go back to their original provider? If the answer to any of these questions is yes, you may have to negotiate quickly.

Second, you should consider getting as much information as you can on the product, the situation, the process, and the needs of the other party. When you are under time pressure, you're never going to be able to do as much research as you would like to, so you have to focus your research efforts. See if you can get in touch with a company that has done business with the other firm in the past. Their experiences may shortcut your research efforts. Normally, when you go into the negotiations, you can expect marathon sessions and comprehensive discussions. In the rapid negotiation, you can expect to find yourself discussing several terms and issues at once. The more information you have on any subject that is likely to come up, the better off you'll be.

Third, draft a plan. Even rapid negotiations don't take place instantaneously. Large scale deals—deals between countries, large corporations, religious groups—are discussed for years before anything is done. Drafting a plan may take some time away from the negotiation itself, but you'll make up this time with your rapid responses to their demands. Drafting a plan also keeps you from making potentially horrible choices, ones below your trip wires. If you have a list in front of you that tells you what you cannot do, you're not going to do it. The general rule is, if you don't have time to draft a plan, you can't afford to close the deal. For every two deals you miss, you'll have saved yourself one embarrassing and financially excruciating situation.

Fourth, divide up the deal into sections and get the other side to agree to talk about each section. This is the only time we encourage segmented negotiations. You want to divide up the negotiation in order to have a set of related concerns to deal with at a single time. In a rapid negotiation, it is easy to lose the focus of what you are dealing with at a given time. It is easy to make concessions that are not in your best interest, and that if you had more time you never would have agreed to. By segmenting, you get a chance to see a whole section of the deal take place and to assess your contentment with that section immediately. Then, when you are done, you can make a rapid evaluation of the fulfillment the whole deal gives you.

If you aren't able to sign the contract, you're probably running out of time. If you have very little time to respond and you've still got problems with the deal, then submit to the other side your best offer as a "take it or leave it." Be prepared to walk away if they reject your proposal. At this point, they know your concerns and you know theirs. If they reject it and suggest a creative alternative, consider their alternative. Always give a deal every chance to get done.

If time runs out and you have had productive talks, see if in any way that time limit can be extended. If it can't, encourage the other side to continue discussions at some future date and keep the relationship as positive and future-oriented as possible. It never hurts to trade all the good will every satisfactory negotiation provides.

X-File #5

The International Negotiation

When you negotiate with a party from another country, you have to acknowledge the difference in negotiating styles and understandings that come from a different historical and cultural environment. In these negotiations, research and investigation are critical to success. Before you step into the negotiating room, get a good feel for the culture of the country you are negotiating in. If possible, find a local person involved in the industry to give you guidance. Your preparation and understanding of the other side's attitude is critical to the outcome of the negotiation.

There are some general areas you may want to pay attention to. In general, you should determine the importance in that country of the status of the negotiator, since some countries determine the seriousness of your intent by the rank of the negotiator. Merely sending a person of the wrong status could doom the negotiations from the start. You should determine the ordinary time frame and pace of negotiations in that country. In most countries, the pacing of negotiations is slower than in the United States (although much of this is changing as the "American" work mentality exports itself across the world). You should determine the location and the structure of the negotiation. Great advantages and disadvantages come with holding the discussions in your country or their country. For example, it may be very expensive for you to negotiate in a foreign country, and you can expect the other side to use that to their advantage. However, if you choose to negotiate in your own home country, you can expect the other side to feel less secure, less comfortable, and perhaps more rigid. Think carefully about where the negotiations are going to take place.

Jane Seymour cut an interesting deal in her negotiations with Aaron Spelling for his miniseries "Crossings," based on the Danielle Steele book. As an avid collector of vintage clothing, she made sure that in her contract she was allowed to keep all thirty-one of the W.W.II costumes she wore during the filming.

Each negotiation with a party that does business in a different country, however, should be individually and carefully researched. It never hurts to learn a bit about that country's history, their economy, their political structure, and the relationship that country has had with your country. Without that information, you might make a verbal gaffe that offends the other side. Most likely you will not use this information during the negotiation. But it is helpful in maintaining a connection with the other negotiator outside the negotiating room. You have shown an interest in their culture and a commitment of your time to understanding it. That can only help your communication transcend the adversarial nature of dealmaking. This information gives you an understanding of what not to do and what not to say during the negotiation. It can also give you a clear understanding of what to expect. If you have the resources, enlist people from the country itself to help you with the task. If you don't, it's time to hit the public library. One magazine that provides a good international overview of events, facts, and business data is *The Economist*, a London-based publication.

Know the facts of the country, know the facts of the company. There is no substitute for information, but you also have to know the unwritten etiquette of the country. For example, in the United States, a good way to offer an opinion on a given topic is to present the information in the form of a question and enlist the other party in helping to solve your problem. In another country, this may not be the case. A question may be seen as a willingness for you to give in on that point and may make the other side even more inflexible about their position.

Let's look at how two diverse cultures require you to adopt different approaches to negotiating. We've chosen the Hungarian and the Chinese negotiators because of the radically different approaches each brings to the bargaining table. We realize it's unlikely you'll ever negotiate with either. But the basic lesson applies regardless—learn how the other person thinks and communicates.

Chinese negotiators like to renegotiate terms after the contract is completed and signed. They view any agreement as first and foremost a partnership between the parties. When they discover that certain terms are creating difficulties for them, they see nothing wrong in adjusting the contract at that time. Let's be clear—they will obey the letter of the contract if required. But the Chinese philosophy holds that the first basis of any agreement is that a partnership exists, and that the terms of an agreement are a secondary facet of the relationship.

It is not unusual to face a Chinese negotiating team much larger than you would find in the United States. As well, the lead negotiator may not be the most important person on the negotiating team. Usually there will be a government representative monitoring the negotiations, although one member of the other negotiating team may wear more than one hat as both a party representative and an employee of the company.

The Chinese negotiation will entail discussion of a variety of subjects without agreement on any specific terms. In fact, to the uninitiated, the initial two-thirds of the negotiation may seem both negative and unproductive. The Chinese negotiator usually gets down to a flurry of details all at once toward the end of a negotiation. If the negotiator begins discussing specifics, that's usually a good sign that the discussions are drawing to a close.

The Chinese are very careful about specific words and statements you make and are not shy about using them to point out inconsistencies in your position. As well, the Chinese are not shy about trying to shame you into accepting their position. Shame is part of the Chinese arsenal.

Hungarians assign a greater value to rhetoric and speech-making than some other cultures do. It is not unusual for the Hungarian negotiator to make speeches of up to two hours long that have little, if anything, to do with the negotiation. Any interruption of this speechmaking is considered rude and could quickly lead to the close of the negotiation.

Hungarians usually negotiate one-on-one, and establish a personal connection with the negotiating representative. They are less comfortable when you come over with a large negotiating team. Expect to spend a lot of time, personal and professional, with the Hungarian negotiator. For them, getting to know the other party and extending hospitality is an integral part of the negotiation. Expect to partake of a lot of Hungarian food while negotiation with a Hungarian negotiator. It is a sign of good will and friendliness that you enjoy and specifically praise the delicacies of Hungary. Look forward to paprika, cabbage, goulash and a lot of hearty food. Trust us—you won't be able to maintain a diet during the Hungarian negotiation.

The Hungarian time frame is unpredictable, particularly because of the forever-impending agreement. You may appear to have an agreement after the first meeting, but expect a number of meetings and conferences. Do not be afraid if some of these meetings digress into emotional negotiating sessions. Emotional overtones appear more frequently in the Hungarian negotiation.

X-File #6

The Telephone Negotiation

In most circumstances, a telephone negotiation is frowned upon. Why? Because you lose all the physical information the other side transmits to you, you lose the ability to make a connection with the other person that would help the relationship, and you'll find that on the telephone, it's easier to turn down other people's suggestions and remain inflexible. Something about the telephone makes each party more sure and more secure in their position and, therefore, more steadfastly dedicated to it. It's nothing personal—it happens to everyone. It's just easier to disagree with a disembodied voice than with a person sitting in front of you. So if you can avoid it, don't negotiate over the telephone.

But if two suppliers you need to negotiate with are located in southern California and northern Maine, it probably makes more sense to use the phone. A telephone negotiation doesn't have to be a disaster. You just have to make certain preparations tailored to a phone negotiation rather than a personal negotiation. Adjust yourself to the telephone negotiation psyche—you aren't going to have any marathon session or entire day to negotiate the contract. Expect and plan on a number of phone calls with rest time to think about creative proposals.

Any phone negotiation will probably take over five phone calls, but you should never have fewer than three negotiating sessions over the phone. The first discussion (or set of discussions) should be informational and comprehensive. Try to identify what the needs of the other party are. Try to identify what they can offer and what they cannot. The more areas of discussion you can identify during this initial conversation, the more creative you will be able to be in your next conversation. Your second conversation (or set of conversations) should involve roughing out the terms of the agreement. Don't be afraid to be creative. Also, don't be afraid to ask to call someone back if they offer something creative you need to think about. One of the great benefits of a phone negotiation is being able to take time out from the negotiation and come back to it without inconveniencing the other party. The third call (or series of calls) should deal with finalizing the terms of the deal and getting ready to put them on paper. After all these phone calls you are going to finally see a document. Take the time to review the document you receive. If it isn't what you discussed over the phone, then the fourth round of discussions begins.

Before you make your first call, however, construct the same negotiating plan you would for a normal negotiation. Write down your needs, your anticipation of the other side's desires, and some creative alternatives you can use to "open up" the negotiation. In this way, your telephone negotiation resembles your other negotiations. Arrange a time that you or the other party will call. Set aside that time as you would for any other negotiation. Make sure all potential distractions and interruptions are taken care of—if being forced to wait in the office while the other party takes a call is annoying, then being forced to listen to hold music while the other side takes a call is just short of insulting.

Next, you should create a checklist of all the topics you want considered. When you discuss a negotiation over the phone, it's easy to let the flow of the conversation take you away from the deal. Once you're done and you are ready to sign a document, you don't want to discover a term that you forgot to consider.

Be careful of the instinct to compromise. Most people discuss terms and come to a basic agreement in the first conversation. A quick decision like that doesn't let you think of the fulfillment level that you get from the deal. Most people think of it in terms of "I can live with this deal." If anything, this book is trying to get you away from just "living" with a deal. Rather, a good negotiation should leave you with a sense of gratification. By letting the negotiation take place over a number of conversations, you get a chance to determine a variety of options that would leave you with a greater sense of satisfaction.

Try to never give the other side a tip for a phone negotiation. It's easier to say no over the phone, so why not use that to your advantage? If the other side wants the tip badly enough, make them pay you back with a different tip. When you're making a deal over the phone, it's hard to know how many phone calls the negotiation is going to take. If you encourage the other side by accepting a tip, there's no telling how many tips you can expect to give up before the negotiation is over. Discourage the other side from that type of behavior. If you don't, expect to give up an average of one tip per conversation.

A final word of advice about telephone negotiations—read the contract very carefully when you get it. Even though both sides agree on the terms, that doesn't mean that those terms will appear in the contract. No one wants to cheat anyone else—lawsuits are great wastes of time and money. Communication, however, may suffer due to the telephone connection.

X-File #7

The Forever Negotiation

When the terms of the deal have long-range implications, you need to take special precautions and keep certain things in mind that wouldn't be a part of a normal, annually negotiated relationship. For example, when you are trying to buy a house you plan on living in for ten years or more, when you are establishing a long-term— three years or more—supplier contract, or even when you are negotiating a time-share vacation home, you must consider things you wouldn't otherwise ordinarily identify as important to the negotiation. Your actions change slightly when you are purchasing a long-term good as opposed to a long-term relationship, so we'll handle one at a time.

The Long-Term Good

When you're thinking of purchasing something that's going to affect your life for a long time, you have to prepare thoroughly and identify what is going to be important to you in the future. It's easy to think of your immediate needs, but more difficult to anticipate future— three-, five-, and ten-year—needs. Part of this is a natural result of the uncertainty of life. Will you have children? What job will you be in? What state will you be in? What will your salary be? So much of the future is uncertain that your long-term needs can be difficult to identify. However, if you find yourself figuring them out with a salesman, you're going to get taken. Negotiating a long-term purchase hinges on the choices you anticipate making in the future, and you have to be as certain about them as you can reasonably be before you start negotiating.

Prepare a range of three possible future directions for your personal and professional life. Identify what you think you will be doing, where you will be doing it, and how much you will make for doing it. Focus on the next three to five years, since it's difficult to predict beyond that. Identify what your primary needs and considerations will be in each scenario. If anything occurs in all three scenarios, circle it. You should look for that in your long-term purchase. For example, if you are shopping for a house, and in all three scenarios you have children, you may need to look for a place with more bedrooms. Identifying needs that are basic to any life you'd end up leading is the object of creating these scenarios. As you identify these needs, you can transfer them to your negotiation plan.

Next, compare those central needs to the good you are thinking of purchasing. If it is a house, does the house seem comfortable and attractive to you? Does it provide enough space and light? Is the wiring sufficient if you intend to work at home? Is the garage large enough if you need a second car? When you negotiate for this property, you can use needs such as these as bargaining chips.

When you come to the table, identify why the other person wants to sell. The more information you have on the pressures on the other side to sell, the better off you'll be. Perhaps the other person has already purchased another home and is under severe financial pressure to get rid of the house right away. If you knew that, would it affect your bargaining position? Of course it would. Do your research to find out why they are selling, what their resources are, and what their history with the product has been. By discussing their experiences with the product, you can gain valuable bargaining information.

Begin with an aggressive offer. You have no idea of the pressures on the other side to sell. Let your bid find out if they have a strong need to take any offer. Stick to your standard negotiating techniques during the negotiation. Make as few concessions as possible while thinking creatively to enhance value in the negotiation. Use your communication skills to your advantage.

One difference you should be prepared for is to be very ready to say "take it or leave it" at some point when you reach a bargaining point of no return. When you are considering a large-good purchase, you have to set limits and be prepared to walk away if you don't get the deal you want. Being ready to walk away is more important than ever when it comes to long-term purchases, because your level of reliance on the product is going to be very heavy. You are not going to get a chance to renegotiate that contract. If you give in more than you would normally on this deal, you have ages to suffer that lack of fulfillment. When you are committing more resources and forgoing other opportunities, you should be prepared to gain greater fulfillment in return.

The Long-Term Supplier

The first thing you must do is determine if you are negotiating with the right supplier. Create a picture of what your needs will be in the future and compare it to the capabilities of the company you are negotiating with. Write down an aggressively successful scenario and a very moderate scenario. If this company and this contract can support either scenario, you are in the right place. If it can't, you need to find another company to negotiate with.

You are going to need to spend more time finding out as much as you can about the company you are negotiating with. Any long-term contract requires as much knowledge about the other party as you have about yourself. Ask them about their size, their plans to expand, the regions of the world they serve. How big is their service department? How many people do they employ? Do they supply any of your competitors? What are some accounts that you can call as references? You are linking your fates through this contract. If they don't recognize your need for lots of information about their company, you don't want to do business with them.

Once you gain more information from the other company and after you decide that their future capabilities seem suited to your future needs, then you want to discuss terms. Treat the negotiation as a normal one with three important exceptions:

1. In the contract, avoid automatic built-in price increases. Inflation has been nominal for nearly the past decade. Over time, you expect the company should get more efficient at making their product. There is little reason you should accept automatic price increases. If you have to include a price-increase clause in the contract, link it to the consumer price index or some other objective scale, so that they cannot pass on operating expenses to you in terms of their goods.

2. In the contract, make certain that failure to perform or failure to pay clauses are explicit, clear, and enforceable. The adage "good fences make good neighbors" applies here. The more straightforward and clear you can be about the terms of the contract, the more

likely each side is to understand and upholds its responsibilities. Particularly in a long-term relationship, you want to be careful that each side understands what it has to do.

3. In the contract, definitely include certain "out" clauses that define situations in which each side may terminate the contract. This is your final chance to identify those situations that might cause you to want to sever your relationship with the supplying company. You may want to include four late deliveries as sufficient grounds for termination, or include the option to terminate if the company's personnel shrinks by thirty percent (which might indicate financial trouble). You have to determine the situations that are important to you. Keep in mind the scale and the ability to service your needs. If one party becomes too large or too small for the other, the relationship may not make sense any more. Consider your "out" clauses carefully.

Pay careful attention to the "out" clauses the other side insists upon. Their actions will tell you what their past experience has been and what their expectations are for the future. For example, if they are very concerned about an "out" clause for non-payment, they may have had a bad experience in the past with clients who did not pay. If they are insistent on putting an "out" clause in if their headquarters moves to another state, you may want to investigate how long they really plan to stay in your region. You do not want to depend on them for a year and a half and then find yourself out searching for a new vendor. You can gain information about what is important to the other side from the out clauses they ask to include.

Understand that while these "X-Files" call for certain tactics, this does not mean you abandon the basic principles of any negotiation. Preparation, communication, and education all contribute to the eventual success of any negotiation. Being aware of the particulars of a situation, however, is how you begin to take control of your deal.

CHAPTER 10

The Handy Guide to the Three Most Common Negotiations

This section looks closely at the negotiations you are most likely to encounter if you aren't a purchasing or sales specialist like most people—car negotiations, property negotiations, and relationship negotiations. There are certain factors you need to know about each so that nothing takes you by surprise when these situations arise. We'll apply the techniques discussed earlier, identify some of the important issues to consider, and offer you certain questions you should ask yourself to make sure you have secured all the information you need before you begin the negotiation. Consider this section a "step-by-step" guide through the negotiation. No book can account for every possibility that may occur in any single negotiation, but the most important issues you can expect to encounter are mentioned here.

THE CAR NEGOTIATION

Normally, when you go to buy a car, everything is stacked against you. There are a hundred different models out there, and a hundred different opinions on each one. Every dealership has a hundred cars in stock, and there are hundreds of dealers. Each dealership has a different relationship with each of its suppliers, and each dealer is under a different degree of pressure to make a sale. Whew.

Do you think the car salesperson needs any more advantage? No, not really. They're doing fine without you helping them. So pick the timing of your deal with care and consideration. When you choose to buy a car is just as important as where in determining price. Traditional dealership sales occur around national holidays, when consumers tend to buy the most cars (based partially on the fact that most car purchases are family decisions and holidays are the only time when a purchaser can gather the whole family together). At these times, car manufacturers offer dealerships incentives to sell their cars. As the manufacturer-to-dealer incentive wars heat up, you can expect the dealers to pass on these incentives to you. These incentives could be a cash payment, financing deals or free options. Looking for a new car around President's day or Christmas can help you find special offers that may make sense for you. If you shop at these times, you should be offered a deal on price, financing or model, if not on all three. The downside of holiday negotiations is that the dealer will have little room to be creative and change the deal to match your needs—they intend to make their money on volume during these periods. They won't offer you the same time or attention shopping at another date might provide.

Timing matters with respect to your old car as well. If you wait until your old car is dead, you are in a much less secure position than when you have a working car at home in the event that you don't make a deal right away. Think of it this way—although most dealers have more information than most consumers, most dealers are also under strong pressure to make a deal. They may have two hundred cars on the lot at any given time, and within months, they have to make room for new models and new brands of cars. If you let the pressure affect them, you're going to get a good deal. However, when your car dies, you turn the pressure back on yourself. All of a sudden, you are under more pressure than the dealer. Also, with a working auto you can always factor into your bargaining session some consideration for the trade-in value of your current car. It is more difficult to assign a value to a car that may have to be towed to the dealer. One car dealership in the Bronx, New York, has their motto on trade-in valuation of non-functional cars painted on a sign outside the lot—"If your car don't run, you get none."

There are many ways to gain advantage in a car negotiation, but you have to plan ahead. You have to prepare, educate yourself, and transmit clear messages to the other side. In most car dealerships, the majority of a salesperson's income is made off of commission. You have to understand what motivates that dealer in his choice of negotiating options. The salesperson's job is to keep the price as high as he can and get the most valuable financing terms possible for the dealership. The salesperson will try to get you to take options that might have a higher mark-up and service contracts that are very valuable to them. The most important thing you have to decide before you go to any dealership is to decide what you want. You'll find you have, if anything, too many choices.

Ask yourself what you need the car for. It seems obvious that you would ask this question of yourself, but once you get behind the wheel of that zippy, black two-door it's easy to forget that you need a lot of trunk room for your kids Billy, Jesse, and Wyatt, and for their hockey gear. Write down not only what tasks you need the car to perform (get to work, pick kids up from school, etc.) but also how much mileage you put on the car in any given week. During the negotiation, you can always point to certain weaknesses in the car's ability to meet your needs as a reason for reducing price or terms. When you are calculating the cost of the car factor in the cost of gas that the car uses, the cost of insurance, and the cost of any service contract. By taking account of the cost of use, you can point out to the salesperson how much the car will really cost you to own and operate. This may motivate the seller to come down on price.

Car dealers have an unusual arrangement with car manufacturers. As an incentive for consumers to purchase their cars, manufacturers provide to dealerships extremely inexpensive financing that they can pass on to their customers. You get in on this good relationship by taking your financing through the dealer. This can result in gains to both you and the dealer. Be sure to keep these as bargaining chips in your negotiation with the dealer—for example, if you are indifferent about two cars, see what kind of a deal on financing each provides.

The most important part of the car negotiation, however, lies in knowing as much about the cars available, the features they provide, the costs of those features and the options available. Getting as much information on pricing as possible is your mission, and you don't have to spend a year reading magazines or read a 700-page book. The world has come far since those days. All you need is a computer with a CD-ROM drive.

The computer revolution has made shopping for a car much easier. You are now able to go into the dealership and argue parts, pricing, color options, and mileage figures like an expert. There are a number of software products that handle this information in an easy and ready-to-digest fashion, like Autoquot-r and Auto Vantage (more on these two later), but one we recommend is the 1995 Auto Almanac. This software product contains information on most of the 1,500 models of cars and trucks that come out every year. The CD-ROM holds hundreds of facts, specifications, photos and reviews of various models by experts in the field. Let's not malign the written word—getting a recent copy of *Consumer Reports* magazine on automobiles is always a good idea. But in buying a car, it is more important to know what not to buy than what to buy.

The computer revolution has simplified the process even further. The 1995 Auto Almanac also has extensive parts and model pricing information and a section on buying tips. All you have to do is put in your needs to the computer and your spending range, and it'll come up with a list of cars that match your needs. It'll even compare their performance on a graph for you, and help you print it out. All of this should be done before you get to the dealer's lot in preparation for your negotiation. Remember, dealers tend to steer you toward what's best for them, not for you. You have to know what options are available and what the pricing differentials are between them.

Once you decide what car (and what options) you want, make a plan. Have a backup car in mind if you can't strike a deal on what you want if your first choice and deal is not available. Particularly in the car negotiation, having a creative alternative in mind works to your advantage. The car negotiation requires a plan, and, above all else, trip wires. If you get corralled into buying the wrong car at the wrong terms and the wrong price, you're going to be paying for it for a long time. Make an aggressive plan and stick to it.

When you get to the lot, you are handling a difficult task—you want to let the salesperson know that you are serious, but you don't want him to think there is pressure on you to buy a car. Be up front with the salesperson that you are serious about buying a car. That should grab his attention. Also, let him know about the models you are interested in. There is no point wasting time. If he tries to direct your attention to another car, listen to him. Is the car more expensive? Does the car give you less fulfillment? You can tell a lot about the salesperson from his suggestions.

You may think in terms of a price range, but always keep it to yourself when you're negotiating anything. A smart salesperson will always get you to buy at the high end of your range. It's much better to give a single price and let the other side work around that figure. If the other side gives you a range, jump right to the top of it. When the other party says, "I'm looking for something in the 50-60 thousand dollar range," you know you've got a minimum of 60 right there.

Don't engage the salesperson in discussing terms right away. Let him educate you about the car. Sometimes you can find more ammunition for your bargaining session in his words. Does he describe something as "standard" that you know is optional? Take your time in the beginning of the negotiation. It will pay off when you eventually discuss terms. Don't bring up the trade-in value of your car until you have gotten a "best price" from him for the car you want to purchase. Then, when you've got him down to as low a price and as inexpensive terms as possible, you can make the deal even better.

When you do discuss terms, keep emphasizing inventive options to the dealer while signaling to him that you are willing to make a deal on positive terms. Once the dealer realizes that with a little work and a little creative thinking he might have a deal, you will see a cooperative effort at working toward a final solution. Car dealers negotiate every business day all day long. If you can talk a car dealer down to your ideal terms, well then, that's the practical equivalent of a Masters degree in negotiating skills. So expect to give a little yourself. But don't back down from your aggressive valuation. Obey the standard rules of negotiation. And, if you aren't able to get a final deal on the terms you want, walk away. There is so much variety and flexibility from dealer to dealer that if you can't get the deal you want in one place, there is a good likelihood that you can get it somewhere else.

If you've had a number of unsuccessful car purchase negotiations, you may want to consider leasing a car. Many car companies have an excellent deal in which they will apply your lease payments to the cost of the car if you decide to buy. If at the end of your lease you decide you don't want to buy the car, then you've avoided the large payments and long-term commitment that a car purchase entails. Of course, the terms of the lease are eminently negotiable. Finding a creative way to get a car deal done is the critical part of a car negotiation, and your entry way to finding these unique alternatives lies in the information you have before you begin negotiating.

If you are negotiating for a used car, you have a different set of concerns that you must address during the negotiation. You are negotiating many of the same terms for a used car as you would for a new car, but you also have to worry about quality and accuracy of information. The most important difference in negotiating for a used car as opposed to a new car is that most often you are not negotiating with a professional seller. Many times, the pressures on the personal car-seller are greater than on the professional car-seller.

You can get a good deal on a used car if you know what to look for. Certain signs can give you information that you can use during the negotiation to get the best deal. Although negotiating for a used car has a higher risk of potential problems, and a higher rate of not working out, the capital required is much lower than other very important investments.

Like most important investments, research can make the difference between having power in the negotiation and being powerless in it. First, find out how long the car's been on the market. That will tell you how competitive the market is for the car. You are going to behave differently if you may not have a chance to purchase the car the next day. Second, look for recent improvements in the car—that's usually a bad sign. People who are intending to sell a car usually take the cheapest and most short-term alternative to a long-term solution. If you see recent improvements in the car, ask if you can talk to the mechanic who did the repair work. Then, when discussing terms, you can use the imperfection of those solutions as bargaining chips.

Find out as much as you can about the other person's plans. Do they plan on moving after they've sold the car? Will you have any way to get in touch with him if he's sold you a lemon? Most used cars are sold "as is" and you as the buyer are responsible for anything that goes wrong after you purchase it. If you can get the other person to certify that the car is in good condition, one thing you may want to consider is if you can pay over time. In that way, you protect against the car not living up to your expectations and spending too much time in the shop. Information in the used-car deal is power, but you have to be careful that the information is correct. The more you know about the condition of a car, the more likely you are to emerge with a fulfilling deal.

Don't forget to research how much it will cost you to get insurance for the car. While most insurance is based on your own driving record and demographic slotting, a portion of it is based on the model and year of the car you drive. When you discuss the price of the car, you may want to bring up any additional insurance cost that may result from your purchase and argue down the price of the car accordingly.

The majority of your research, however, should be based on the car itself. There are books called "blue books" which give the value of a car based on mileage, options, model and condition. Once again, a fantastically liberating machine, the computer, can help you with all the information you need. Two online services are the most widely known computer aids in researching used cars. The first is called Autoquot-r (pronounced "Auto-quote-er") and is available on such online services as CompuServe (Go Aq) and Genie (Autoquot-r). This service provides not only new sticker price information but also "blue book" information that tells you how much a car manufactured in a certain year, that specific model and with a certain amount of mileage, should bring. All the perks, colors, EPA mileage ratings, dealer invoice costs and average percentage markups are included in this information database. It provides a breakdown showing standard and optional equipment, and what is available for every model. Autoquot-r can mail a report to you by the next business day. By keeping vast records of most models from 1972 on, Autoquot-r can do much of your information gathering for you and provide you with a valuable objective report that you can point to during your negotiation.

The second service is called Auto Vantage, which you can get to through Delphi (Autovantage) and Genie (Cars). Aside from the same information Autoquot-r provides, Auto Vantage also provides trade-in and selling price, recall history, and tips to make you a better bargainer. The club claims an average saving of $2,000 per car. Auto Vantage also offers discounts on products, auto shops, and auto-service centers. Even if you aren't negotiating a used-car purchase, you might want to look into the benefits that Auto Vantage may give you on your car service. The important thing to take into the negotiation from Auto Vantage is the specific pricing with which you can argue your point. People price their used cars based on what they hope to get. If you can let someone know that the market is pricing her good much lower, you have more ammunition.

All this information will only help you during your bargaining sessions. Treat it as a normal negotiation, but argue your price and your terms aggressively. If someone is selling their good secondhand, they're looking to get rid of it as soon as possible at a price they can live with. The "can live with" price is usually much lower than the "hope to get" price, which is usually the advertised price. For many secondhand cars, the pressure on the seller is greater than the pressure on the buyer.

The car negotiation obeys the standard rules of negotiating, and is usually played by those without very much information. The greater information one group can get, the more power they have during the negotiation. Car negotiations can go well for you—you just have to be very confident that you know more than the other party, and you have to be aggressive in your valuations and creative in your thinking.

THE PROPERTY NEGOTIATION

The property negotiation is the most likely negotiation you will face in your life. You may not always need a car, you may not always be in a relationship, but you will always have to live somewhere. And if you ever start your own business, you may have to lease space in an office building, space in a mall, or a plot of land. Property negotiations occur all the time, but you don't have to fall into most of the traps other people do with these deals. Other people panic, chase their own offers, and don't plan their negotiations properly. You, on the other hand, have more skills and knowledge than those people do. By preparing completely, you're going to emerge from the property deal more fulfilled than the next person.

Property negotiations fall into two major categories—renting and purchasing. Whatever your needs and your desires, your negotiation skills can get you through the most difficult waters. Just remember that liking and wanting the property is only one function of how happy you are with the deal. The rest depends on your dealmaking skills.

Renting

When renting from a landlord, the first thing most people do is to decide if they want the space or not. Usually, that decision is based on aesthetic and locational concerns—what does it look like and how convenient is the location? While these are important considerations to keep in mind, you can't divorce them from the terms of the deal. As in any negotiation, the more you know about the value of the entire deal to you, the more you can adjust your offers to reflect that deal.

Before you begin to discuss terms, make sure you've done all the research you need. For example, you may have looked at the place and found it meets your locational and spatial needs. Some other questions you want to ask yourself might be: Have you looked at the neighborhood? What are comparable apartments in the neighborhood renting for? What are the terms in those leases? Does the area provide all the services you are going to require? A supermarket? A drugstore? A dry cleaner? Have you interviewed the neighbors or other tenants in the building? What has their experience been as residents of the building? How is parking in the neighborhood? Has the landlord taken care of repairs or improvements in a timely fashion? What renter's insurance do most of the tenants in the building use? You can ask the insurer if there have been any claims from that building for burglaries or break-ins. These may seem like a lot of questions to ask and a lot of research to undertake, but each one gives you more of a chance of getting the deal you want on the space you want. The answer to every one of those questions can become important in previewing how the negotiation is going to progress. If you know what the other side is going to use to support their figure for rent on the space, you need to know what you can use to attack it.

You want to know as much as you can about your landlord. While interviewing the neighbors and talking with past tenants is helpful, you also want to do some independent objective fact gathering. Make a call to the Better Business Bureau (or your local equivalent) to find out if any complaints have been logged against him. How big is your landlord? If your landlord manages a number of buildings, how much attention does he spend on this one? Does he live in the building? You don't want to find out that he spends very little time at your building on the coldest night of the year when you have no heat. What are your landlord's concerns? You may be able to figure those out by asking local real estate agents or through preliminary discussions with the landlord himself. By knowing what history and concerns your landlord has, you can find creative, interesting ways to allay those concerns.

Two medical real estate negotiations tell the worst and the best of lease negotiation. Dr. Jean Howard, an oncologist from Yuba City, California, found out she had to pay her rent while called away for the Persian Gulf War. She had forgotten to include a clause in her lease stating that in the event that she was called to duty the lease would be terminated. On the other hand, Dr. Robert Bernard Moorhead negotiated a lease in which the rent increases or decreases based on the volume of patient flow. Both Dr. Moorhead and his landlord benefit from this creative arrangement—the true measure of a successful negotiation.

Did you find the apartment through an agent? Can the agent lobby on your behalf? Rental agents pose a dilemma. Whenever you have to go through an agent, you end up having two negotiations. The first one concerns you and the agent—some figure based on the value of the agent's services to you. One thing you should discuss is all the things the agent can do for you. Is the agent going to negotiate the lease for you? Sometimes that's a bad move. Sometimes it's a good move. You have to know what kind of reputation and relationship this agent has with this landlord. How much access does the agent have to good rental properties? How flexible is the agent on payment and terms? A smart creative alternative you can suggest is to link your payment to the agent based on performance. In that way, the terms of that agreement can be structured to your maximum benefit.

The second negotiation you will have is the one with the landlord. Unless you have an agent in an unusual position of strength or with an incredible reputation, you want to negotiate for yourself. You have learned a great number of negotiating skills—never be afraid of using them. You can get a better deal than most people.

What do you know about the time frame of the negotiation itself? Does the landlord want to do it in one sitting? Does it take place in their office? In the location itself? If you are going to ask the other side for some unusual changes to a lease, are they going to have to ask their boss for that change? In that case, you may choose their offices as the location. Are you going to suggest some changes in the lease in return for improvements in the apartment? It might make sense for you to hold the negotiations in the location, then, so the landlord can begin to picture what you plan on offering. These considerations are all things you have to take into account before you begin to discuss the terms.

Is anyone else involved? Are you suggesting a co-tenancy with another party? There are benefits (from a negotiating standpoint) and detriments that follow from involving another party. The benefits come from being able to point to the strengths of either party in being able to allay the fears of the landlord. For example, if the landlord is concerned that one party may not be able to pay the rent on a space, bringing in another party may make the rent seem more likely to be paid. Additionally, some apartment landlords like to rent to pairs of people because they tend to take more care of the apartment than lone renters. However, suggesting a co-tenancy can also multiply your problems. If one tenant has a problem with another tenant, the landlord will feel wary of the stability of the proposed co-tenancy. Having a partner in a negotiation can also be a difficult task to manage, particularly if you have differing valuations of the space. You must identify your areas of disagreement and prepare a plan before you meet the landlord to discuss terms. Otherwise, you run the risk of transmitting mixed messages to the landlord and undermining the trust you'd like to develop.

Finally, inspect the location and see what opportunities are available for you. Some suggestions for improvements that you can use as bargaining chips:

- You can offer to paint the place yourself.
- You can offer to do small repairs.
- You can offer to upgrade the security in the location.
- You can offer to replace old built-in equipment or appliances.
- You can find another tenant to fill any vacancies in the building.
- You can offer to upgrade a common area.

Every location has its unique features that a tenant can use in the bargaining discussions to his advantage. By finding these features and exploiting them as creative alternatives during the negotiation, you can get more value out of the deal. For example, one construction firm operating out of Morristown, New Jersey, struck an unusual deal with their landlord. They took occupancy of one floor of a three-story office building and paid a rent of $100 per month for the first twenty months. In return, the construction company built, at cost, a parking garage on the lot next door to the building. The garage raised the building's value and was a bonus for many existing tenants in the building. The landlords were able to raise the rent of the other tenants and still provide a service worth the price. By being creative about what you can offer the landlord that costs very little to you but means a lot to him, you can find that elusive win-win scenario that is hiding out there.

When you choose to rent, you also should be careful about what rights you negotiate into the contract and what rights the other side negotiates into the contract. Standard clauses exist that outline the most common reasons a landlord can break the lease and the most common responsibilities the tenant has. Unusual clauses have to be added to a standard contract, so be wary when a renter asks you to put in a "standard" clause. Sometimes these clauses will work only to your disadvantage. You should treat them like tips—small terms to be traded during the negotiation. Be careful about including in the lease any automatic increases in rent. Some buildings are zoned that way and there is nothing you can do. But if you have to have some increase in rent, make it an increase that makes sense. You would rather link it to some inflationary measure than to a blanket percentage increase. Usually, a good measure of inflation can be achieved by linking it to the percentage change of the consumer price index. Special cancellation clauses are dangerous to let the other side negotiate into the contract. You are basically saying that they can cancel your lease at any time—imagine the potential upheaval and cost of such a situation. If they insist on including a cancellation clause in the contract, make them pay for it with as many concessions as you can. One thing that you can do is to request that any cancellation clause, if invoked, requires that the landlord pay the relocation expenses of the tenant. This suggestion often makes landlords think twice about invoking those clauses. Make certain that any penalties or payment dates are clearly spelled out. For example, "the beginning of the month" is a phrase that we use all the time. But does that mean the first? Is payment by the fifth still the "beginning" of the month? Be precise and specific about your dates and your payments. You won't regret it, and neither will the other party.

Gary Willensky, crazed psychopath and former girls' school tennis coach, negotiated an unusual lease that should have raised a red flag for the landlord. Willensky got absolute privacy, to the point that he never met the landlord, and kept all the utilities and bills in the landlord's name. He wanted no records that would trace him back to the cabin, and he paid a year's rent in advance in cash. When he tried to kidnap a former student and bring her to the cabin, the motive behind his request for privacy became obvious to everyone.

Purchasing

Because of the various legal situations encountered in purchasing a space for commercial use, this section is primarily going to consider purchasing a home or apartment. The general approach you should have is one you can apply to buying any expensive good: Research, have a plan, use techniques, and be ready for creative adjustment. All of those stages should be part of any negotiation for property or another expensive product negotiation.

A property purchaser must be careful about more things than a renter. After all, your relationship will go on, theoretically, for a much longer period of time. The commitment of your resources is much greater. Your options also are more limited—after all, you can't offer to fix up the house if the seller will come down on price, as you would in a rental. Once you buy, it's all yours—all the cracks you didn't see, the mice you didn't hear, and the leaks you didn't notice. But just because there are dangers in the deal, that doesn't mean that you have to be a chump about the negotiation. If you prepare well and stick to a careful plan, you can come out ahead.

Preparation is the key to a property purchase negotiation. The more details you know about the property and, in particular, the more you can pinpoint the seller's position, the more likely you are to be able to get a great deal. Again, the problem that most people have is that they see and love the property, then make one bid after another, higher then higher still, not recognizing that a little shrewd bargaining could have garnered them much more happiness with the deal. Research the property as thoroughly as you can. Sometimes the location will be perfect, but the property won't be well maintained and will have problems. For example you want to find out if there is any history of property disputes or liens against the property. This will tell you what to expect from your neighbors or old creditors. Do you want to find out about the leaky sewage system one week after you move in? Preparation and research will avoid most of these problems. You want to find out about:

- property values in the neighborhood
- environmental concerns in the neighborhood
- additional pluses/faults of the region (shopping, schools, industry, location, travel, community, etc.)
- the neighbors (length of residence, history of disputes)
- the building/structure (financial, historical, state of repair)
- the trend of the market (purchases in the region/sales in the region)
- the motivation of the seller (extremely important!)
- the alternative plans of the seller (if you are able to discover them)
- financing (local bank, your own funds, provided by the seller)
- closing costs (who pays? how much?)
- repairs before sale (what you can ask for, what you expect to get)

Inspect the location with an engineer if you can. Look at the foundation, the structure, the heating system, the driveway, anything that might require a large repair bill in the immediate future. Any areas of concern you have can end up being points for your side in a negotiation. You can either use them to knock down the asking price or you can offer to have the other side make those repairs to your satisfaction before the sale. When inspecting the location, try to have as specific and clear a vision as possible of what the place will eventually look like when you are through. This will help you explain during the negotiation your set of desires. Once your ultimate vision of the property is stated, the other side may be able to help you with your negotiation problems. For example, perhaps you want to turn an apartment with three small bedrooms into an apartment with two large bedrooms. You can bring that up during the negotiation as a reason you can't spend more money on the apartment—that you have to keep money in reserve for those renovations. This puts the other party in the position of coming up with creative alternatives that satisfy your desires while staying within your own limits. The more you know about what you are purchasing and what you want from it, the more prepared you are for the negotiation.

Last, find out as much as you can about the seller. Do your best to figure out what pressure they are under to sell their home. Do they need a larger house? Every day they spend in the old, smaller house puts more of a strain on them to sell. Have they bought another home already? They have a very short time-frame to sell their house, then, since two mortgages are more painful to pay than one. Are they moving to another state or city? Sometimes a job opportunity forces a family to sell an excellent house at below-normal value. Do they need money immediately? The more you can identify the pressures on the other side, the more likely you are to get the deal you want. One particular gauge you can use to identify the position of the seller is: How long has the place been on the market? What price did it initially go on the market at? What price is it at now? Knowing the selling history of the location can help you a lot. It affects your approach. If you see a place you are interested in the day that it comes on the market, you are going to write down a different plan than if you like a place that has been on the market for two months. Talk with an agent or the seller about their experience with the house. Sometimes you can gain valuable information.

Next, write down a plan. This plan should be an anticipation of the negotiation, including your trip wires. Write down all the potential bargaining chips that you have. By seeing the range of possible outcomes unfold on your page, you make it more likely that you can avoid the worst ones happening to you in the real negotiation. Anticipate the time frame of the deal as best you can in your plan. See if you can use the timing of the deal to your advantage. Do you know when the other side plans to move from the house? Do you know when their mortgage payments are due? Do you know how anxious the other side is to sell? Use your knowledge of pressure and how it affects a deal to get you many of the terms you want.

When you are purchasing a house or building, however, it's especially important to avoid bidding against yourself. Let's say a house is up for sale at a price of $100,000. You make a bid of $79,000. The other side rejects that bid. You should not come back with another, higher bid until you have more information on why the other side rejected your offer (and their saying "too low" is not enough information). Let the other side come back to you with a bid of their own or a discussion of some ways to creatively satisfy both parties. It is important to realize that most real estate agents work for the party that owns the house. They are not there to get you the lowest price possible. Speak directly with the sellers if you can. Keeping communication open and productive between the sides only helps you. If you can't speak directly with the principles involved, make sure you transmit messages with your behavior. Make bids that are more creative but clear and precise.

Your behavior during the negotiation is worth being careful about. For example, visiting the property a number of times sends the message that you're serious and interested. This can work to your advantage if the other side doesn't believe you to be interested, or to your disadvantage if the other side believes you are so interested you will definitely offer more money for the property. What message do you send if you bring a contractor or decorator to the location? If you don't answer the other party's messages for a week? If you spend ten minutes looking at the property? Consider your actions carefully— they can make the difference between an 'alright' deal and one that leaves you smiling and feeling good.

A useful resource available to the private property purchaser is the Robert Irwin book *Tips and Traps About Buying/Selling Your House*. Irwin takes on in detail the most important concerns you should be careful of before you decide to buy or sell, and discusses the negotiation and what to watch out for during the deal itself. Irwin's first chapter heading is "Everything is Negotiable," and we know that's right. The details of your negotiation, however, should reflect your own situation. Choose your arguments and your positions with care. Negotiate based on your knowledge and your needs, not on any arbitrary system of value.

One smart thing you may want to do is put yourself in the position of the seller. It is a difficult decision to sell a house. It is aggravating to have people walk through your house, asking questions and assigning their own value to your property. The negotiations are not always pleasant and more often than not, they don't lead to a deal. How can you use this to your advantage? The other party is going to be pretty happy when they sell the house. By raising their expectations that a sale will go through, you can encourage them to be flexible in their valuations. Encourage the other side with your positive commitment to the negotiation and be very hard on the terms. Sometimes, a little positive vision can gain you a lot.

THE RELATIONSHIP NEGOTIATION

You may not have thought of this, but your newfound negotiating skills can make all the difference in your personal relationships.

The relationship negotiation is the trickiest, diciest, and most interesting of all negotiating scenarios. Why? Because it takes place all the time and because it has enormous ramifications for your general level of fulfillment with your life. The arguments that take place in any relationship are forms of communication. Some fail, some are successful, but all could be shortened by obeying the simple rules of negotiation. The greater your negotiating skills, the more positive and happy you are going to be in your relationships.

The first thing you have to do is to expect the appropriate attitudes from each other. Going into a relationship expecting the other person to convert completely to your interests and your lifestyle is like going into a business negotiation expecting the other side to acquiesce to your needs—they won't, and if they do, you didn't get as good a deal as you should have. This doesn't mean that you should not profess your needs clearly and positively. In fact, that is your only chance of setting up the appropriate expectations in a personal relationship. Set down up front what is important to you. How you convey this information is critical to keeping the relationship positive and productive. Encouraging the other person to take an interest in your interests is a good way to face these conflicts. But you have to show an interest in theirs, and you have to be willing to accept that they may just not really enjoy, say, debating politics as much as you do. By setting up this groundwork of positive and mutually encouraging communication, you can stake your interests out without excluding the other person's interests.

When you have conflicts, as usual, phrasing problems in the form of questions can be a helpful means of getting beyond the disagreement. As in a business negotiation, you want to state your problems with the idea that together, you can come to some creative solution to the problem. By phrasing these disagreements in the form of questions, you invite your significant other to not only contribute ideas but to solve the impasse. Opening up conflicts to unforeseen solutions leads to "win-win" situations that keep a relationship fresh and intense.

There is one downside to phrasing conflict in the form of a question. Eventually, you begin to sound like a therapist, definitely not the tone you want to set for your long-term relationship. Any long-term relationship relies on continued fulfillment. Every single examination of difficulty within a long-term relationship doesn't reveal the full range of your emotions and the range of your involvement with each other. While most often compromise is important, you want to keep strong about the things that are important to you. Occasionally, you want to battle it out. And conversely, strategic losing is a good idea. Not every solution is perfect. Not every solution is available. However, if you choose the things that are important to you and encourage the other party to stick to what is important to them, you both can be happy while differing in opinion.

In a relationship, more than in anything else, creative alternatives are important. In anyone's life, there are a limited number of possible things to do, places to go, ways in which to spend time and money. Being separate people, it is likely that at some time, the two of you will come into conflict in your relationship over one or more of these issues. By being aware of creative alternatives, you increase the likelihood of finding some way to satisfy both people. Let's take a simple example. You like going out to dinner, and your partner likes cooking at home. You might come up with the idea that the two of you cook for a picnic and take it somewhere beautiful to eat. The more in touch with your ingenious alternatives you are, the more chance you have of succeeding in your personal relationships.

Like all long-term agreements, eventually, a relationship develops some degree of trust. You should make an effort in every step of the relationship to encourage trust. Trust fosters communication. Communication leads to greater mutual awareness. Awareness and creativity lead to agreement. If all this sounds familiar, it should—

the issues of professional negotiation enter pretty smoothly into the sphere of personal relationship negotiation. The principles of behavior, intention, and creativity can be found at the center of any good relationship, whether between supplier and contractor or boyfriend and girlfriend.

There's one big difference, however. Traditional negotiation tactics are a bad idea in a personal relationship negotiation for one obvious reason: Most of the tactics are designed to discourage honesty and encourage a specific response from the other party. Over time, all tactics lose their effectiveness and only encourage ire. The fundamental center of personal relationship negotiations is trust, and using tactics erodes trust. Remember that you are on the same side as your partner! Just as in a business relationship, it's better to build up rather than break down trust, so the personal relationship negotiation should always be geared toward cementing and building on trust.

Transmitting non-contradictory messages is the most important thing to do in your personal relationship negotiations. Communication breakdowns result from sending mixed signals. Nothing causes more stress in a relationship than confusing someone about your needs or intentions.

A Final Word

Every real-life negotiation is going to have its own unique twists, and it's up to you to navigate those turns as smoothly as possible. You've learned the skills that make the top dealmakers able to drive a harder bargain—now it's up to you to put them into practice. Negotiate at least one thing every day. It doesn't matter whether it's what movie to go to with a friend or a six-movie deal: The same principles apply. Be confident, firm, and observant, and you'll find that every day you get more of what you want.

CHAPTER 11

The Negotiation Arena

The Negotiation Arena gives you a chance to test all the negotiating skills you've accumulated through the last ten chapters. Each arena matchup gives you and a competitive partner a chance to take different sides in a negotiation and try to strike a deal. Read only the information for one party. Then write down your negotiation plan and pass the book on to your partner. When you're both ready, the two of you can hash it out.

Send your best results to *Don't Be a Chump!*, The Princeton Review, 2315 Broadway, New York NY 10024. You may be mentioned in a future edition of *Don't Be a Chump!*.

SCENARIO ONE: RUMP PLAZA

Player 1:

You are M. Pickney, accountant, and you and your Collie, Alonzo, are considering renting an apartment in Rump Plaza. You have been shown three apartments. The first apartment is a studio with a utility kitchen (a hot plate, a sink, and a microwave), one window, and beautiful wood floors. The apartment is small and needs painting. The last tenant paid $900 per month. The second apartment is a one-bedroom apartment with a full kitchen and many windows on the fiftieth floor of the building. The floors are in bad shape, the wiring appeared suspect, and a strange odor permeated the entire fiftieth floor. The one-bedroom apartment was offered for $1,200 per month. The last apartment was a large one-bedroom apartment on the tenth floor featuring a marble sunken bath, a walk-in closet, twelve-foot-high ceilings, and a small terrace overlooking Central Park. It was offered as a "steal" at $1,950 per month.

You and Alonzo have been together ten years, and you will not part with Alonzo. You are a gourmet chef and enjoy cooking. You have few possessions and can move in as soon as you sign a lease. You would like to live in Rump Plaza because it is close to work, close to Central Park (where you can walk Alonzo) and a highly prestigious building. You have been informed by the renting agent that one week from now, most, if not all, the available apartments will have been rented. You have a basic understanding of repair work, but are by no means an expert. You have been at your job as an accountant for five years with the same firm and expect to stay at that firm for the rest of your career. You have $3,000 in cash saved in the bank and make $3,500 per month after taxes. You are looking at these apartments with the idea of living alone (except for Alonzo).

Player 2:

You are the renting agent for Rump Plaza. You have been renting apartments for one year here, and your job is nothing but a headache. In building the highly leveraged structure, Mr. Rump's contractors apparently cut some corners and used some substandard materials. There is no danger to any tenant, only a continuous flow of repair requests and complaints. As a result, more and more tenants are choosing not to renew their leases. You, as the renting agent, are under pressure from the owner to fill those open apartments. Soon.

You have met M. Pickney and would like him to be a tenant in the building. You are wary of his ability to meet the rent obligation, and are therefore desirable of getting a security deposit of two months' rent from him. You understand the building's prestige, but you also understand that in a few months, when more apartments open up, the building's reputation will suffer. You would like M. Pickney to sign a two- or three-year lease committing him to stay in the apartment. You have discretion to offer any apartment for at least $800 but if you offer either of the two larger apartments for under $1,000 and $1,700 receptively, you can expect some complaint from the owner. If the apartments remain vacant for two months, however, it is likely you will be out of a job.

You have an overworked maintenance staff, and understand that a "foul odor" that no one seems to be able to locate has permeated the fiftieth floor. You understand that M. Pickney has a dog, and although your standard renters agreement includes a "no-pets" clause, exceptions have been made in the past and you have no problem with allowing one more tenant with a dog in the building.

Scenario Two: Supply Contract

Player 1:

You are B. Drainy, the supplies manager for the offices of Do-Rite Gardening Supplies. You have been charged with purchasing all the office supplies that Do-Rite uses in any given year. Do-Rite employs over two hundred office employees, all of whom need supplies. You currently purchase paper, paper clips, rubber bands, and printer-ribbons from four different suppliers. You pay $12 per ream of paper, $0.50 per box of 100 paper clips, $0.65 per box of 100 rubber bands, and $11.95 per printer ribbon. You send your office truck to pick up the supplies at each location when you order more.

You are entertaining a bid from a new potential supplier who has no track record in your state, but has been operating in a neighboring state for years. Their reputation is for inexpensive products, which sometimes are late in delivery. You are unhappy with your current suppliers because they all offer different terms of payment and the multiple coordination of shipment pick-up has lead to more than one office snafu. You are under pressure to find a single supplier for all office supplies. And, as always, you are under pressure from above to reduce your costs.

Player 2:

You are Z. Milliken, head salesperson for Arrival Office Supplies. You have been assigned to the company's first attempt at breaking into a neighboring state. This is the first meeting your company has had with another company in this other state. Your bosses are putting pressure on you to close a deal and announce your entry into this new market. Since you have no track record in this state, you are authorized to sell goods only marginally above cost. Your cost structure is as follows:

- Paper: $8 per ream
- Paper clips: $0.48 per box
- Rubber bands: $0.70 per box
- Printer ribbons: $10.40 per ribbon
- Notepaper: $1.02 per pad
- Delivery charge: $.03 per item

You cannot, however, go below cost on any single item. You have had some problems recently with the quality of your goods. Your own factories are producing some of the least expensive goods on the market, but at a cost in quality. Your company plans to address the quality issue, but not until next year.

You would like to have a four- or five-year deal, but you are empowered to accept a deal of any significant duration.

Scenario Three: The Movie Theater

Player 1:

You are the owner of a movie theater in Beaumont, North Carolina called "Lights and Action." You own the theater and the plot of land the theater rests on. Your mortgage payments on the land and theater and average film distribution deals total $3,500 per month, including any land taxes. You originally paid $22,000 for the land and theater. The theater grosses from $3,000 to $8,000 per month, depending on the movie and the season. You have owned the theater for ten years, and, for better or worse, it has provided you and your family with a good livelihood and a good working environment. You enjoy the atmosphere of the movies, and enjoy the connection with the variety of people who come to see your movies. You are well known in the community and have a good reputation.

You have been approached by Nakatori Cinema Corporation, who want to buy your theater from you. They have offered you $100,000 for the entire parcel, including the land. They want you to decide in five days if you accept or reject their offer. Recently, the cost of movies from studios have gone up and you can picture your monthly bills extending to $4,000 or more.

The Nakatori Cinema Corporation has a reputation for coming into small towns, buying all the local cinemas and then raising the price for all the theaters in the town. Nakatori has taken over the other two theaters in the city and you are worried that if you do not sell, under pressure from the large corporation your profit margins could be eroded or, in a worse case scenario, disappear.

Player 2:

You are the local representative for the Nakatori Cinema Corporation. Your company owns 850 theaters worldwide, and you are in charge of purchasing new theaters. Your company has successfully pursued a policy of entering a small town, purchasing all the towns theaters, and coordinating the entire town's showing of movies. Part of the company's strategy depends on purchasing all the theaters and coordinating showing within six months of entering a town. Five months have passed since you purchased your first theater in Beaumont.

The strategy is less successful when one theater in the town is not absorbed by the corporation. These "rogue" theaters have successfully managed to galvanize support in each town they exist in by lowering prices, showing competitive movies, and organizing local citizens against the Nakatori corporation. You are under pressure to make Beaumont a success. You have invested $250,000 already in two local theaters. Now, only "Lights and Action" remains as the local alternative.

You are authorized to spend up to $400,000 in any given town and licensed to hire any townspeople as employees of the corporation at competitive wages. You are allowed to buy space, rent space, lease space or sell space, but your mission is to convert the town in the manner of the Nakatori strategy.

Scenario Four: The Soccer Star

Player 1:

You are the agent for Pedro Macherato, the Italian League's famous soccer star. Your client, who speaks little English, is known for the strength of his legs and the flamboyant playboy lifestyle he leads. A media favorite, Pedro is also a consummate professional on the soccer field. He seems to become a better player the more pressure he is under. Last year, at a charity event, he kicked a football through some American football goalposts as a stunt. He scored a field goal at a distance of seventy yards. This started him thinking about becoming a professional football player in the United States.

Pedro has spent the last three months working with a personal trainer on how to become a professional place-kicker. He has three scouts who claim "he might be the best ever." However, no professional soccer player has ever successfully made the transition from soccer star to football star.

Pedro has had a number of injuries related to soccer, but is basically in good health. He has decided that he is going to play football in the United States no matter what next year, but only the two of you have that information. He has been offered publicly a one year, one million dollar contract to play soccer in Milan. Your client doesn't know if football will work out—he craves the adventure. He wants to take a risk.

Pedro is thirty years old, and he has an ex-wife and three children, the oldest of whom is nine years old.

Player 2:

You are the official negotiator for the Jacksonville Jaguars, a new team in the National Football League. Your team, while very high in expectations, is likely to suffer for the next three to four years from a lack of talent. You could use a gimmick, to keep the press and the fans occupied while you bring together a group of football players who can be competitive in a professional league.

The National Football League operates under a salary cap, which prevents teams from spending over $43 million dollars per team. Bonuses, however, do not count toward the salary cap, nor do incentive payments for reaching specific levels of achievement. Currently, the Jaguars maintain a salary of $42.6 million dollars.

Pedro Macherato is an international figure whom the Jaguars feel will not only attract non-football fans, but will also help with their merchandising of Jaguar paraphernalia in Europe, a projectedly booming market. In the absence of signing Macherato, they will hold local try-outs in the hopes of signing a local favorite.

Macherato has requested a two-million-dollar per year contract, an unheard-of figure considering he has no record in professional football. However, the NFL record for the longest field goal ever is 66 yards. Macherato has already surpassed that in practice. The media excitement surrounding these negotiations has made the Jaguar fans practically rabid with anticipation of getting the best place-kicker ever.

You are authorized to spend anything that keeps you under the salary cap, but less than one-point-two million dollars overall. You are also authorized to offer specific English language and media training to endear Pedro to the press. The owners, however, are concerned that Pedro will violate team rules, lead his playboy lifestyle, and embarrass the Jacksonville Jaguars. If you feel that he will not take the sport seriously or obey his commitment to the team, you are instructed to politely and tactfully extricate yourself from the negotiations.

Scenario Five: The Car Deal

Player 1:

You are in the market for a new or used car—you don't care which. You just want to get the best car for your money. You have a bankroll of three thousand dollars and, if you need to, you would be able to support payments of $237 per month. You like the color green. You could live with a two-door or a four-door car. You don't care much about mileage.

You do care, however, about reliability. You are a uniform purchasing specialist for local hospitals, schools, and security guards. You must travel from location to location, inspecting wear and tear on uniforms, taking surveys on their satisfaction, and looking at new plants. Your very job depends on having a functional, functioning car.

Currently, your car is dead. It is sitting in your driveway, waiting to be towed to the junk yard. You've been told by experts to give it a funeral. You have been renting a car for a week. You need a car desperately.

Player 2:

You are a car dealer at the Samuel B. Smertz Car Emporium, and this month, things have been a bit slow. Very slow. As a matter of fact, you need to make a sale badly, or your job is in jeopardy.

The Smertz Emporium sells both new and used cars. The dealership makes more on used cars, but tends to sell more new cars. You sell either, and you've currently got two cars on the lot that could make up for a very bad month. The first car is a new, two-door Mazda Miata. It gets forty miles to the gallon and is cherry red and in impeccable shape. It also costs $13,000. The second car is a used car that has been sitting on the lot for weeks, taking up space. It is a dirt-brown Chevy Nova that gets twenty miles to the gallon, and has a history of motor problems. It costs $4,900.

Company policy is to get as much money as possible up front, but at least a minimum of twenty-five percent of final purchase price. Every dealer is allowed to negotiate the price of any car within twenty percent of sticker price. However, the salesperson's commission is determined by the final sales price of the car.

On new cars, the dealership can offer financing of three percent annually. On used cars, the dealership can offer six percent annually.

The dealership keeps a crew of maintenance personnel (mechanics and technicians) on staff to prepare the cars for sale, for customization, and for fixing newly acquired used cars for resale.

SCENARIO SIX: THE INTERNATIONAL NEGOTIATION

Player 1:

You are Anna Merican, chairperson of Paul Revere Industries, a major cosmetics manufacturer located in Alexandria, Virginia. You are negotiating in Moscow, Russia with a newly formed company called American Beauty, which plans to market cosmetics for men and women in Russian urban centers. You are one of a number of cosmetics companies that are trying to establish a larger presence in the former Soviet Union. A deal that makes you a presence in Russia would be a big coup for your company and for you personally. You know that American Beauty is negotiating with other cosmetics firms. If no contract agreement is reached, then you will be around six months behind your competitors.

Your cost structure is as follows:

Blush	$0.30 per unit
Lipstick	$0.72 per unit
Nail polish	$0.92 per unit
Base	$0.20 per unit
Moisturizer	$1.20 per unit

Each product is subject to an import surcharge of $0.55 per unit and the best shipping rates you can get is $0.22 per unit from Alexandria to Moscow.

You have no knowledge of the marketing systems or structure of business in Russia. You will rely completely on your partners to handle the details of Russian sales, but you would like to be able to bring in an independent auditor to monitor the sales of your product. You also want to be able to sell your old inventory which no longer has a large market in the United States. You want a long-term contract to establish your presence in Russia.

Player 2:

You are Mikhail Checkhov, chairperson of American Beauty, a company you began two years ago located in Moscow, Russia. While you have spent the last two years trying to finalize arrangements with many cosmetics manufacturers, you have only gotten the rights to license European cosmetics and resell them under your name. You want a real American supplier so that you can capitalize on the current rage for everything American in Russia. You have a meeting scheduled with Paul Revere Industries, which, so far as you know, has no other Russian distributor. You are willing to pay fair rates because you feel you can sell these cosmetics at a large mark-up. Your planned pricing structure is as follows, assuming the current exchange rates remain constant.

Blush	$2.95 per unit
Lipstick	$2.25 per unit
Nail polish	$4.00 per unit
Base	$2.25 per unit
Moisturizer	$2.80 per unit

You would like to pay in rubles as opposed to dollars, because it would take time and effort to convert your rubles to dollars, and you would rather let the other party assume the risks of exchange rate fluctuations.

As well, you have an agreement with the tariff authorities that states that while other firms may pay as much as $0.55 per unit of import, your firm will only have to pay $0.35 per unit. You also have reserved any extra space on food freighters that ship from the United States every month. While it takes two months for the ships to complete their voyage, your shipping costs are $.06 per unit.

You would like to negotiate an exclusive agreement, but you have to do it quickly. The current desire for everything American can be expected to last another two years, and after that, the market is uncertain.

Scenario Seven: The Stereo System

Player 1:

You are Madison Smart, a Wall Street executive, and you've just walked into Drake's Electronic Castle, an electronics store near where you work. You've gone here because you've been recommended to this place by your boss, who said the salesperson was "a pushover." Your boss paid $3,000 for his stereo system.

You have an old, functional stereo system at home that you are tired of, although it still works. You are looking for a receiver, a CD player, a tape player, and a set of speakers. However, if you can only find some of the components now, you do not feel the need to purchase them all at once. You must, however, purchase a new set of speakers. Without those, the rest of the system is useless.

You have $1,700 to spend for the whole system. You have excellent credit and can pay over time. You have a big date next Saturday night, and would like to have the stereo in place by then.

You also want to look good to your boss, so you feel the pressure to get a good deal for your money. After all, how would it look if you got taken by a "pushover?"

Player 2:

You are Sal Mansales, the salesperson for Drake's Electronic Castle, and you are in charge of the stereo section. A couple of weeks ago you made a great sale to a guy—a $900 stereo system for $3,000—but since then, you've had bad luck and not many sales. The money in your bank account is dwindling. You have promised to take a friend to a fancy Italian restaurant next week, and anticipate that will cost you $300. You need a sale, and you need a sale fast.

Your pricing structure is as follows:

Goods	Cost of Goods	Marked Price of Goods	Your Commission
Receiver 1	$375	$675	$150
Receiver 2	$425	$750	$200
CD Player 1	$250	$400	$75
CD Player 2	$250	$375	$50
Tape Player	$100	$215	$40
Speakers 1	$80	$99	$5
Speakers 2	$195	$300	$40
Speakers 3	$125	$299	$50

You can reduce the price of any good, but it comes directly out of your commission.

You also have available to you a service contract for each piece, which guarantees full support for three extra years that costs $35 per contract. You get $20 of that $35 dollars.

SCENARIO EIGHT: THE FOOTBALL TEAM

Player 1:

You are Magnus Larson, the owner of Larson Cable Television, and you want to purchase the Montana Raiders. The Raiders are the football team you grew up watching. When you were a child they won two Superbowls. In the last thirty years, however, they haven't won any.

You know the Raiders are for sale, and you want to make an offer. The team's owner also owns the Montana Dome, the stadium the Raiders play in. The dearth of fan support and the lack of a television contract has lowered the price on the team. That's why you decided to try to get them now.

You want to purchase the team and broadcast them on your own network. You have plenty of money on hand—$100 million in cash and a line of credit at eight percent for another $350 million. Your analysts have valued the team and its merchandising rights at $58 million. The stadium, a multi-purpose domed facility, is valued separately at $82 million. The team's payroll is $34 million dollars per year, and the management costs another $7 million to support.

You want to bring the team back to the level of its glory days. You feel the old owners, while wanting to keep that Montana Raider spirit, have let some young prospects go too early and not changed with the times. You want to win and win now. You want the team. Period.

Player 2:

You are Doug DeJeffries, current owner of the Montana Raiders. Your family has owned the team for twenty-nine years, and seen it through the good times and the bad times. Recently, the bad times have outweighed the good times. You are in a financial pinch. If you do nothing, you will miss a payroll payment to your players and employees in two months.

Your payroll is $34 million with another $9 million in administrative and ownership costs (including your $2 million annual salary). Your team, through an internal audit, was recently valued at $42 million dollars and the stadium known as the Montana Dome (although it is officially titled the "Doug DeJeffries Sports Complex") is valued at $51 million.

You have tried everything to get a national television contract and ways and incentives to promote fan support of the team, but six losing seasons in a row have soured the potential revenue sources for the team. You have been advised by your accountant that "it's not a question of if you have to sell the team, it's a question of when and for how much."

You want to see the team do well. Your family name is associated with the team itself, and even if you sell, the team holds a special place in your life.

SCENARIO NINE: BERMUDA, BAHAMAS, COME ON PRETTY MAMA...

Player 1:

You are Mel, and you have been going out with Flo for three years now. You are discussing taking a vacation and the two of you disagree on where to go. You want to go to the Bahamas and Flo wants to go to Bermuda. You don't see much difference between the places, except that the Bahamas are cheaper and allow gambling. Other than that, they are two sunny islands with nothing to differentiate them.

This conflict happened the last time you two decided to go on a vacation. You wanted to go to Las Vegas and she wanted to go to Sedonia, Arizona. You gave in and went hiking, horseback riding, visited local museums and dusty, old restaurants that wouldn't have passed a single board of health inspection. You were miserable and so was she.

You've been to the Bahamas before and know what to expect. The food is a little bit expensive and Americanized, the music is pure pop from the States, and the beaches are small and rocky but clean. The weather is good and you could expect a few relaxing days. The Bahamas, as well, are cheaper by about $30 per person per day, although once food is included, that difference is eliminated.

You know more about what you don't want than what you want. You don't want anything with "flavor." You don't want anything with "local crafts." You don't want anything with the word "quaint" attached. You want to go to the Bahamas.

Player 2:

You are Flo, and you have been going out with Mel for three years now. You have gone on vacation with him before, and while sometimes it has worked out, there was one notable failure in your past: Sedonia. Mel wanted to spend a week in Las Vegas, a city that you find nothing attractive about. You don't gamble. You don't like gambling. But Mel doesn't seem to recognize this.

Sedonia was recommended to you by a friend. You went there expecting the feel of the Grand Canyon with wonderful food and a welcoming, non-touristy group of locals. In fact, you stayed at some unpleasant places, ate awful food, and had terrible weather. It was a disaster. You are the first to admit that.

You want to go to Bermuda. You have been there before and seen the beautiful beaches, the quaint, small cottages, and the peace of mind that the island inspires. The seafood is fresh and inexpensive, and the whole pace of the island is much more relaxed. There is no gambling, which Mel doesn't like. He wants to go to the Bahamas. The one time you went to the Bahamas was over Spring Break when you were in college. The music was non-stop, the drunken people stumbled over you on the beach—it was a nightmare. You came out of the vacation with no rest, no quiet, and no fun.

You value peace. You value your relationship. You want to go to Bermuda. You don't want to go to the Bahamas.

Scenario Ten: The Wolverine

Player 1:

You are Lefty McClure, and you're in the market for a wolverine. Sure, you've heard they are dangerous, unpredictable animals who often turn on their masters in a violent, bloody fashion. Sure, you've seen the photographs. But your three-year-old girl wants one and you promised to get her one. So here you are.

You've met this wolverine before. Her name is Shana, and her current owner has had her for three years. Shana is nine years old, and is expected to live to the age of twelve. Shana is blind in one eye but has an excellent sense of smell, as far as you've been told. She spends most of her time sleeping and eating, but you've seen her walk around the yard. She seems nice. Very peaceful.

The owner is planning on retiring soon and wants to make sure that Shana is taken care of in case he decides to move. You have $300 to spend on Shana, all the gear, all the shots, and food for the first two weeks. Above that, you can not afford the animal.

Player 2:

You are Gary G. Moore, and you own Shana, the wolverine. You won her in a poker game. And you've lived the last three years in constant fear.

You didn't think a wolverine would be any different from a wolf. Until you saw it attack your car. It tore a door off with its paws and teeth. Ever since then, you've kept it in a fenced-off area and thrown it food when you had to. But you haven't always had to. Sometimes you wake up at night and hear it howling. Over the past three years, four neighborhood dogs have been reported missing. You've never even found a single bone. The next morning, Shana is always normal, as if nothing happened. Except she's full.

You've got a chance to sell the wolverine, and you plan to grab it. You want to get $300 (the cost of two weeks' food) and the other person can have everything else. You have a leash, some fencing, sixteen frozen chickens (Shana likes chickens), and some medicine you put in the chickens to keep Shana healthy. Recently, Shana has been going blind in both eyes. She is still dangerous, though. She is also getting mean.

You can't afford not to make a deal, but you want to get as much money as you can.

CHAPTER 12

Answer Key

NEGOTIATING WORKSHOP #1:

Test Your Skills

(p. 15)

1. Exhibited a lack of awareness of the other party's needs.
2. Reacted inappropriately to a poorly received offer.
3. Bid against himself.
4. Needed to educate each party on importance of certain issues.
5. Lack of communication apparent.
6. Didn't acknowledge different systems of value.
7. Showed a lack of preparation.

NEGOTIATING WORKSHOP #2:

Preparing a Negotiating Plan

(p. 27)

Doug and Kathy's Negotiating Plan:
The owner needs:
- headliners in his show
- stability of headliners
- to not pay too much and bankrupt the show

He will ask for:
- a two-year contract
- $500 per show each

They will offer:
- to trade length of the contract for more money or vice-versa
- to trade free promotional appearances and plugs for more money or deal length
- to get married in the ice show for promotional purposes

The owner's Negotiating Plan:
Doug and Kathy need:
- more money
- more stability
- more recognition that they are stars in the show and great performers

They will ask for:
- five-year contract
- $1,000 per show

He will offer:
- a three-year contract for $700 per show
- to trade length of contract for money or vice-versa
- more money for guarantees of performance
- to increase their billing and promotion
- an "out" clause in the event they want time off to have children in return for an agreement to tutor and train any replacement skater for free

NEGOTIATING WORKSHOP #3:

Preparation Checklist

(p. 29)

1. Babs
2, Yes
3. $600-$700
4. Delayed Payment, gear included, medical costs covered
5. Several exist, including leasing the pet
6. 4/4
7. The danger of the wolverine
8. The promise to Gabby's children

Negotiating Workshop #4:

Communication Skills Exercise

(p. 45)

1. D	6. E
2. A	7. D
3. C	8. E
4. B	9. B
5. B	10. C

Negotiating Workshop #5:

Playing Dumb

(p. 57)

1. The scope of the agreement can change (both in terms of items and geography).
2. The price is linked to the longevity of the product, which is not a factor in what paper clips you purchase.
3. The increase in price is due to research and development of the product, not an increase in raw material cost, the only cost that you should allow to be passed on to you.
4. The data on which this is based is going to be provided to you, so you will have that as a bargaining chip.
5. The terms of the relationship extend over ten years— it's time to make them "renew" their relationship.

Negotiation Workshop #6:

Strategic Education, No Extra Information, or Referral to Third Party?

(p. 62)

1. Strategic Education
2. Strategic Education
3. No Extra Information
4. Third Party
5. No Extra Information

Creativity Exercise #1:

(p. 65)

1. You could put cotton in the ears of the guards then break the fishtank with the hammer. Or you could put cotton in the ears of the guards then reach unprotected into the fishtank, so the guards would not hear your screams of agony.
2. You could put your arm through the steel canister and reach into the water.
3. You could wrap your arm in the towel and reach quickly into the water for the diamond.
4. You could suck the water from the tank with the straw then pluck the diamond quietly from the tank.
5. You could hang the beef over the tank to attract the piranha and bat them with the baseball bat as they jumped for the food, then retrieve the diamond.
6. You could use the hammer or bat to "sedate" the guards, then break the fishtank.
7. You could use the cup to scoop the fish from the tank and then get the gem.
8. You can do anything else you can think of. If you have a great solution we haven't thought of, send it to the address listed in the Negotiation Arena (chapter 11). We'll consider publishing it.

NEGOTIATING WORKSHOP #7:

Careful Listening

(p. 73)

1. 9	6. 0
2. 2	7. 0
3. 7	8. 2
4. 1	9. 6
5. 4	10. 8

NEGOTIATING WORKSHOP #8:

Increasing Options

(p. 76)

1. Size of car contract.
2. Substitutes for the vehicle.
3. Terms of payment.
4. Length of the relationship.

NEGOTIATING WORKSHOP #9:

Taking Time

(p. 85)

1. Yes, most likely	6. Yes
2. No	7. No
3. No	8. Yes
4. Yes	9. No
5. No	10. No

Negotiating Workshop #10:

Identify the Tactic

(p. 91)

1. Upping the Ante
2. First Draft
3. Higher Authority
4. Pressure Cookers
5. Fact or Fiction?
6. Exhaustion
7. Side-Issuers
8. Rotating Negotiators

9. "Take It or Leave It"
10. The Beggar
11. The Non-Negotiator
12. Good Cop/Bad Cop
13. The Staller
14. Or Else
15. The Tip

Negotiating Workshop #11:

Using the Question

(p. 94)

Any question you write that gets across the message in a non-insulting way is correct. Don't let anyone tell you there is only one way to convey information.

Negotiating Workshop #12:

Assigning Value and Trading

(p. 103)

1. Artistic Control
2. Length of Contract
3. Producers
4. Promotion

NEGOTIATING WORKSHOP #13:

Keeping on Top
(p. 117)

1. Yes	6. No
2. No	7. Yes
3. Yes	8. Yes
4. No	9. Yes
5. Yes	10. Yes

About the Author

Nick Schaffzin graduated from Stanford University in 1990 and received his Masters degree from Columbia University in 1995. He is the author of *Reading Smart: Advanced Techniques for the Intermediate Reader*, published by Random House in 1994. He has been teaching and writing for The Princeton Review since 1992. He loves negotiating. He recently traded an old rag and a small bag of dirt for a large island off the coast of Malta.